BENN'S WORLD HISTORIES

The Emergent Continent

Africa in the Nineteenth Century

ERIC HALLADAY

NEW YORK/ST MARTIN'S PRESS INC 1972

© *Eric Halladay 1972*

All rights reserved. For information, write:
St. Martin's Press, Inc., 175 Fifth Ave., New York, N.Y. 10010

Printed in Great Britain

Library of Congress Catalog Card Number: 72–86499
First published in the United States of America in 1972

Affiliated Publishers: Macmillan & Company, Limited, London
– also at Bombay, Calcutta, Madras and Melbourne –
The Macmillan Company of Canada, Limited, Toronto

1 West-African figure of a man firing a gun

Contents

Maps

2   A nineteenth-century engraving of a Zulu village

The African Context

THE HISTORY of nineteenth-century Africa was until recently seen mainly in terms of increasing European involvement in the continent with the scramble and colonial rule as the ultimate finale. The European contribution is, of course, a significant part of the story, but to emphasize it unduly does scant justice to a number of events where the initiative lay largely with the Africans themselves.

When the Europeans talked about the 'Dark Continent', they gave a distorted and misleading impression of Africa, but it had nevertheless some basis of truth. The continent was for the greater part of the nineteenth century in a state of flux. The Europeans witnessed inter-tribal conflicts and cruelty, slavery and depopulation, and they convinced themselves that these were the natural order of things in a barbaric and unfriendly continent. A few, like the German explorer, Heinrich Barth, saw, beneath the surface confusion, the basic virtues of African society and tried sympathetically to understand what was happening.

The opening decades of the century saw the end of what had been a relatively stable period in African history that had lasted more than a hundred years. The changes that took place were in some cases closely intertwined with external events such as the ending of the European slave trade and the steady penetration of East Africa by Arab merchants. But there were other events, notably the extraordinary consequences of the rise of the Zulus in southern Africa, that had their origins in Africa itself. The force of these changes was often cataclysmic and few parts of the continent escaped their effects. The result is a history of often bewildering complexity but one in which the vital decisions more often than not were being taken by the Africans themselves. The imposition of European rule between 1880 and 1914 superficially suggested that almost a century of crisis was over. In practice, however, this was far from the case since the African response to colonialism was to lead within a single lifetime to further change as new nation-states gained their independence.

5

Generalizations about the people of Africa at this time need to be treated with caution. Practically everyone was involved in some form or other with agriculture, although geography forced considerable variations. Pastoral farming, mainly cattle, was most common along the broad swath of territory stretching from the area of Lake Victoria to the Zambesi and beyond into the central and eastern parts of southern Africa. Among the Sudanic peoples, a mixed system of cattle, corn, barley, and rice was developed. Any form of pastoral farming was impossible in the forest areas of the Congo river system and West Africa where the often scanty produce of man-made clearings was supplemented by hunting and fishing. Local tradition too played its part. The nomadic Masai of East Africa, for example, were forced into becoming highly specialized cattle farmers since they believed it was wrong to take anything from the earth.

The characteristic organization was the tribal village or the extended family group. The customary law governing these communities was complicated and often of great antiquity. With deep roots that had the long sanction of primitive religion, these codes of law were invariably sensible and responsible. They dealt with landholding, cropping, and the care and maintenance of each tribesman so that practically every village had a rudimentary social security system.

Most African villages were fairly self-contained and isolated from each other but this did not prevent the growth of a number of all-embracing political and economic systems. In most cases these were to be found round the central areas of trade, particularly when there were contacts with the world outside Africa. Mineral deposits were especially important here since the Africans had long had the skill to recognize and exploit them. South of the Zambesi there still stand the impressive stone remains of Zimbabwe, the site of the great gold-producing empire of Mwenemutapa during the fifteenth and sixteenth centuries. By 1800 the focus of attention had moved further north into the region of the rich copper deposits of Katanga. It became the centre of a vigorous commerce spanning most of Central and eastern Africa.

The growth of urban communities in Africa was slow but where they did exist they always indicated the development of long-distance trading. Down the East African coast, a number of Arab towns had been built through contact with Arabia and to a lesser extent with India. More famous were the cities of the Sudan such as Timbuktu and Kano, while further west the forest states had copied them on a smaller scale. Trade in western

3   A sculpture from the Lower Congo of
two Africans carrying a European in a hammock

Africa had always been more vigorous than in the rest of the continent. Salt
from the coast had long been exchanged inland for iron and gold. The
leather work of the western Sudan was already well known in southern
Europe by the close of the Middle Ages. But outranking all other forms of
commerce was the slave trade to the Americas which only ended in the
middle of the nineteenth century.

   The effect on the African peoples of the changes that took place after
1800 is difficult to gauge. For many this was clearly considerable, leading
to serious dislocation of normal life. This was certainly the case in eastern
and southern Africa once the full effects of the Arab slavers and the rise of
the Zulus were felt. At the same time it is probably easy to exaggerate the
extent of these calamities among people who had for centuries been accustomed fatalistically to accept the natural disasters of crop failures and
animal pests. The resilience of the Africans to events beyond their control
probably allowed them to recover fairly rapidly from the dramatic events
of the nineteenth century. To the average farmer, there was only a fine
distinction between invasion by an unknown enemy and the effects of
famine and disease.

4   In restoring their royal authority, the emperors
of Ethiopia relied on the traditional authority of
the Coptic priesthood and a strong organized army.
This lithograph shows a priest and a warrior of
about 1860

1 The Sudanic States

ONE POSSIBLE DANGER facing the historian of nineteenth-century Africa is the temptation to compare unfavourably the tribal systems of the rest of the continent with the more sophisticated Islamic states to the immediate south of the Sahara desert. There was more than one European who would have agreed with Sir Richard Burton's claim that when he came into contact with Islam he was relieved to hear 'once more the voice of civility and sympathy'. Burton was an unrepentant admirer of Islam but such an attitude did less than justice to the often complex character of tribal life among the pagan Africans. His bias, however, did emphasize that these Sudanic states stood in a different tradition from the other areas of tropical Africa. Their possession of written records might alone have differentiated them, but as important was the fact that they were heirs to a great religion which during the greater part of the nineteenth century was increasingly hostile to traditional African paganism as well as to European influence. Its effects were felt far from the Sudanic region, reaching down East Africa as far as Lake Nyasa and the basin of the Zambesi.

These Sudanic states lay along a narrow belt of grassland south of the Sahara that stretched from the Senegal river to the mountains of Ethiopia. Their inhabitants treated the Sahara as an inland sea, being prepared to risk the long journeys by camel and horse across the desert to trade with the Mediterranean lands of the Maghreb.

Except for the isolated Christian empire of Ethiopia, all these Sudanic states had been influenced by Islam, adding strong cultural and religious links to the commercial ones that already existed with the Ottoman empire. In the not too distant past some of them had been vital centres of Islamic learning but during the eighteenth century much of the enthusiasm had been lost and the influence of paganism had correspondingly increased.

This decline in religious zeal was also reflected in the growing political instability of these states. In 1770, James Bruce, the Scottish explorer, visited one of them, the sultanate of Funj, and he was not impressed. 'War and treason', he wrote, 'appear to be the only occupation of this horrid people.' By the early 1820s, Funj was in fact to be absorbed by Muhammad Ali's forces advancing down the Nile from Egypt, but its weaknesses both of religion and politics were common to most of the Sudanic states at this time.

Ethiopia

The Christian empire of Ethiopia was no exception to this. By 1800 the emperors, from their capital at Gondar, had failed to hold their ancient state together. Provincial rulers and warlords established virtual independence and fought a series of disruptive civil wars against the emperor and each other. In an attempt to save the situation, the late eighteenth-century rulers enlisted the help of the pagan Galla tribesmen whom they had been fighting in the southern part of Ethiopia since the sixteenth century. But

5 A Galla queen and her sons. A loose union of pastoralists, the Galla were formidable warriors and were a major cause of Ethiopia's weakness at the start of the nine-teenth century

the only result of this fruitless alliance was to establish paganism at the heart of the Coptic Christian empire. Bruce on his journey found little more to please him among the Ethiopians than he had at Funj. 'I at last scarce ever went out,' he wrote, 'and nothing occupied my thoughts but how to escape from this bloody country.'

But in spite of Bruce's pessimism, Ethiopia grew in strength during the nineteenth century and was able by its close successfully to resist European attempts to conquer the country. Today, Ethiopia is unique in Africa, its monarchy and church being able to trace their origins as far back as the ancient kingdom of Axum in the second and third centuries A.D. No other African state has institutions with such a long and continuous history.

This is one reason for Ethiopia's survival. Its ancient cultural and political traditions proved in the end tough enough to withstand the anarchic conditions that existed before Theodorus II (1855–68) became emperor. He was the first of three important emperors, the others being Johannes IV (1871–89), and Menelik II (1889–1913) whose reigns were to be decisive in reuniting the country and resisting foreign invasions.

Internally, their most important task was to revive the almost forgotten authority of the monarchy itself. All of them were hampered in this by their relatively weak claims. They became emperors more by their military strength and their standing in their own provinces than by their royal blood. Theodorus, a cruel and neurotic man, was the least successful but he faced by far the most difficult problems. His greatest achievement was to plant in the minds of many Ethiopians the idea of a united empire with a strong emperor at its head. He was assisted in this by the Coptic Church whose ancient traditions had proved strong enough not to be totally lost during the crises facing Ethiopia since the middle of the eighteenth century. As a youth Theodorus had spent part of his time in a monastery and there is no doubt of the sincerity of his religious zeal. He restored churches and altars in the area he reconquered, while his fierce hatred of the pagan Gallas and all Muslims harnessed the priesthood to his cause.

Johannes and Menelik were able to transform Theodorus's idea of a strong empire state into some form of practical reality. By 1900 the influence of the Galla had been finally removed, the church had become the throne's firmest ally, while awkward provincial governors were replaced by generals loyal to the emperor. As a symbol of the new régime the capital was removed in 1887 to Addis Ababa and within twenty years was connected to Jibouti on the Gulf of Aden by a railway. Some headway was made with encouraging overseas trade which in turn enabled the emperor to increase his income through taxation. Not only did this allow the administration to improve but it enabled Ethiopia to present a more respectable face to the outside world. Less than a hundred years earlier one emperor's treasury was so bare that there was not even enough to cover his funeral expenses.

The building of a new capital and of one single-track railway did not mean the end of the difficulties facing Ethiopia. There were still areas where the emperor's authority remained weak and tenuous as late as the 1930s. Nevertheless, the domestic achievements of these rulers were impressive, but no more so than the manner in which they resisted a number of powerful external enemies. The Ethiopians were not blind to the European world and were anxious to learn from it. As early as the 1840s they had allowed the establishment of British and French consulates and these representatives were cautiously welcomed as were a limited number of Protestant and Catholic missionaries. They presented the Ethiopian authorities, however, with some novel problems of diplomatic protocol. When in 1860 some tribesmen killed the British consul, Theodorus merely compounded the felony in European eyes by pouncing on the culprits and killing and mutilating some 2,000 of them. The British were even more convinced of the barbarity of the place when a few years later Theodorus imprisoned the new British consul with some of his friends. He took this step because he was irritated at the Foreign Office's oversight in not replying to his friendly letter to Queen Victoria and because he suspected the British of encouraging the Egyptian forces on his northern frontier. When they failed to obtain the prisoners' release by peaceful means, the British in 1868 sent an Anglo-Indian army under Sir Robert Napier. The unfortunate Theodorus, recognizing the inevitable, sent a last pathetic message to his people:

> Believing myself to be a great lord, I gave battle; but by reason of the worthlessness of my artillery, all my pains were as nought . . . I had intended if God so decreed, to conquer the whole world . . . You people, who have passed the night in joy, may God do unto you as He has done unto me.

Disraeli rejoiced in the fact that 'we have hoisted the standard of St George on the mountain of Rasselas' but it did not stay there for long. The only fruits of conquest that Napier wanted were the captives and after their release he withdrew.

6   A highly dramatic European view of the death
of Theodorus in 1868, after Napier's victory

The Napier expedition was important since it suggested that Ethiopia could be easily conquered. During the 1880s and 1890s, at the height of the European scramble for Africa, both France and Italy began to take an increasing interest in its affairs. In 1889, having failed to gain a foothold by negotiation, the Italians decided to invade. But they were unable to repeat Napier's success and at Adowa in 1896 Menelik won a decisive victory that finally established both the unity and independence of Ethiopia.

What the Italians and others had ignored was the degree of administrative reform that had taken place in Ethiopia and the extent of the country's rejuvenation under the three emperors. In the shaping of this recovery, foreign policy and war played an important part. Their long isolated history and the nature of their religion meant that Ethiopians saw their foreign policy in something like crusading terms. It was a role that the emperors genuinely enjoyed and accepted.

7   The Emperor Menelik and his chiefs after their victory over the Italians at Adowa. Their success was partly due to the use of rifles supplied by the French

During the 1860s and early 1870s, Egyptian expansion down the Nile had reached the Gulf of Aden and the undefined boundaries of Ethiopia. The Egyptians had absorbed with comparative ease the former Sudanic states of Funj and Darfur and had pushed westwards into Wadai. Their forces were well equipped and, after Napier's easy victory, must have seen Ethiopia as a fairly easy victim. In 1875, after a number of preliminary skirmishes, they made a determined attack on the Ethiopians from north and east. Johannes, however, surprised the invaders with the skill of his defence and was able to halt their advance. As a result the northern frontiers of Ethiopia were secured and more clearly defined by treaty.

The Egyptians were only too happy to see the end of this particular quarrel since they were faced by increasing unrest in their Sudanese territories. In spite of the efforts of Europeans like General Charles Gordon to bring order to the area, Egyptian rule remained harsh and inefficient. During the early 1880s the Egyptians in the Sudan collapsed in the face of a determined religious and national movement led by Muhammad Ali, the *mahdi*, the Saviour of the Muslims. Driven by a burning desire to introduce into the Sudan a more pure form of Islam, the *mahdi* was aided by his main lieutenant and ultimate successor, Khalifa Abdallahi, who combined religious zeal with considerable gifts as an administrator. The Sudan soon became an energetic, militant, Islamic state, the more dangerous to its neighbour since it was efficiently run.

Since Abdallahi claimed many of the territories on the Ethiopian border that the Egyptians had been disputing, war with Ethiopia was inevitable. Johannes IV was killed in one of the battles, but his rival and successor, Menelik, continued the vicious struggle. Although unable to win any decisive victories, the situation moved slowly in favour of the Ethiopians. They had prevented any serious inroads into their territory while at the same time Abdallahi's control in the Sudan began to weaken under the strain of the war. The final blow, however, against the mahdist movement was struck not by the Ethiopians but by the unholy alliance of British and Egyptian forces under Kitchener at Omdurman in 1898.

By the end of the century Menelik was sufficiently secure to encourage Ethiopian expansion into the pagan lands to the south and east, an advance that forced many of the native Somalis southwards into the dry and barren lands of what is now northern Kenya. By 1900, not only had Ethiopia been secured and reunited but it had even taken its own modest part in the scramble for Africa.

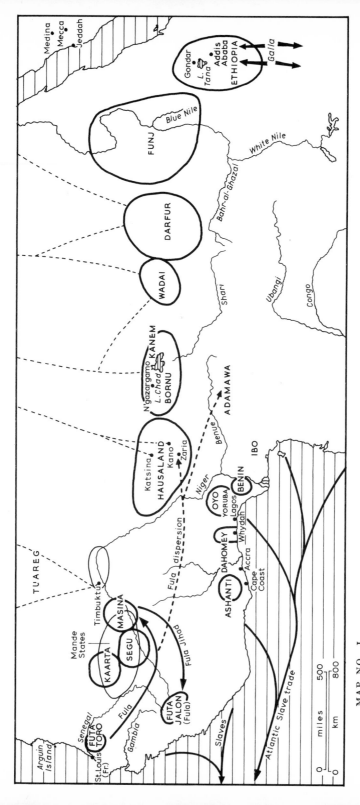

MAP NO. I
Northern Africa in 1800

The Central and Western Sudan

During the nineteenth century the central and western Sudan experienced a religious and political revival as dramatic as Ethiopia's. The effects of these changes can still be seen in many parts of the area today, but, although they led to the foundation of some large and important new states, they were not after 1880 strong enough to resist the full force of French and British expansion.

The states affected by this recovery stretched in an arc from the Lake Chad region to the Senegal river. By far the most united was the ancient empire of Kanem-Bornu. At its height in the sixteenth century, Bornu had dominated a wide area round Lake Chad. By 1800 it was no longer as strong. Its kings or *mais* had lost control of the trans-Sahara routes and its military power, based on fast-moving cavalry, was declining. The atmosphere of the court at the capital of N'gazargamo was one of ostentatious luxury. Nevertheless, in spite of these weaknesses, Bornu remained the most civilized and cultured of the Sudanic states. This can largely be explained by the important part played by Islam in its political and social life. Justice and administration were conducted according to Islamic law and the precepts of the Koran, while its rulers, even Ali ibu hajj Hamdun (1750–91) who produced over 300 male children but lost all his battles, were invariably devout and literate.

Immediately to the west of Bornu was Hausaland, a collection of city-states of which in 1800 the most important were Katsina, Kano, Zaria, and Gobir. Constantly fighting and skirmishing with each other, none of them had ever been quite strong enough totally to control all Hausaland. As early as the first half of the sixteenth century, the Hausa had felt the impact of Islam although it never established the same hold as in Bornu. In each of the cities there were influential Islamic groups but over the years they had been forced to come to terms with paganism many of whose practices they had absorbed.

What distinguished Hausaland from its neighbours was the extent and variety of its manufacturing and trading interests. These included finely woven dyed cloth, leather goods, brass, pewter, and above all slaves. In return, imports included silks, spices, and perfumes from North Africa, salt from the coast, and gold and goora nuts from the Ashanti. The constant inter-city wars seem hardly to have discouraged this vigorous commerce

17

that enabled the Hausa to seize control of the Sahara trade from Bornu, which was left to the less skilled business of capturing slaves. The products of the area and the reputation of its craftsmen were well known outside Africa. In 1791 the recently formed Africa Association in London tried unsuccessfully to establish direct contact. It had been encouraged by an account of a visit to Hausaland during the 1780s by a Moroccan Arab, a summary of which was published in its *Proceedings*:

> ... In his rude unlettered way, he described the government as monarchical, yet not unlimited; its justice as severe, but directed by written laws ... For the probity of their merchants, he expressed the highest regard ... In passing to Houssa from Tomboctoo ... he found the banks of the Niger more numerously peopled than those of the Nile from Alexandria to Cairo; and his mind was obviously impressed with higher ideals of the wealth and grandeur of the empire of Houssa than those of any kingdom he had seen, England alone excepted.

To the north-west of Hausaland were the heirs of the great Islamic empire of Songhai that had once stretched from Senegal across to and beyond Timbuktu and down towards the northern area of what is today Nigeria. In 1591 Songhai had collapsed in the face of the superior armies of Moroccan invaders. By the end of the eighteenth century the remnants of those victors still clung precariously to the region around Timbuktu, constantly fighting the Touareg and other tribesmen of the surrounding desert. On the western side of the Niger bend the former Mande-speaking subjects of Songhai had after many years built up a number of states of which by 1800 the two most important were Segu and Kaarta, largely pagan but increasingly coming under Islamic influence.

The most interesting and soon to be the most influential people of Sudanic West Africa were the Fula (or Fulani). A mainly pastoral tribe, their original home was Futa Toro on the southern bank of the lower Senegal river. Over the centuries these people had become dispersed over a very wide area as they searched for new grazing grounds even reaching as far east as Darfur.

Many of the more far-flung Fula were still in 1800 pagans. But Futa Toro itself had accepted Islam during the sixteenth and seventeenth centuries and one of the Fula clans, the Torodbe, became influential missionaries and preachers wherever there were Fula settlements. In Hausaland in particular, many Torodbe accepted urban life and began to revive the traditional Islamic scholarship that had once flourished in the western Sudan.

18

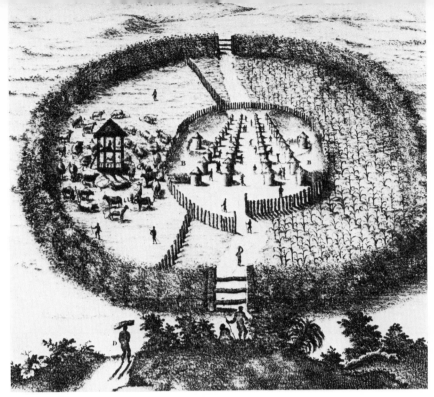

8 A typical settlement of the ubiquitous
Fula. The crop is maize, introduced by
the Europeans

Futa Toro and Masina, a Fula-governed state on the Niger bend that became independent on the fall of Songhai, were to be the main bases for the extraordinary Islamic renaissance of the late eighteenth and nineteenth centuries.

Militant Islam

The great religious movements that swept over the Sudanic states during the nineteenth century were part of a wider puritanism that was making itself felt throughout the Islamic world. During the eighteenth century, in the heart of Arabia itself, the fierce and dedicated Wahhabis had reformed many of the older religious brotherhoods and inspired new ones. The rising of the *mahdi* in the eastern Sudan was part of the same revival and there were similar outbursts in the Maghreb.

9 The blood-stained banner of the *mahdi*,
whose *jihad* led to a revival of Islam on
the banks of the Nile, menacing both
Ethiopia and Egypt

In the western Sudan, the leaders of militant Islam shared the sincere
belief of all such reformers that they alone represented all that was true and
good in the faith. Since the collapse of Songhai, Islam had been forced to
come to terms with many of the pagan beliefs and practices of the area. It
became a tolerant religion, adopting many non-Islamic characteristics. The
reformers certainly exaggerated the extent of these lapses to justify their
own puritanical creed. They failed to recognize that one reason for the
survival of Islam in the west had been its mildness and ability to adapt. But
by 1800 there was a growing number who felt that the period of compromise should end and they were prepared to use in their cause the final
Islamic weapon, the *jihad* or holy war.

The *jihad* was a duty prescribed in the Koran and blessed by the Prophet
himself. To the serious Muslim, the world was divided between the 'Abode
of Islam' and the 'Abode of War'. Those fortunate enough to belong to the
first were obliged to try to convert those in the second, using the *jihad* if

other methods failed. Over the centuries this simple theory had become complicated by bitter theological debates about the exact meaning of a true believer. Extremist reformers normally accused those Muslims unable or unwilling to share their strict creeds of having abandoned the faith. It was on these principles that the western *jihads* of the nineteenth century were conducted. Muhammad al-Tunisi, an Egyptian religious teacher and physician, explained the motives of the Fula extremists in 1810:

> They accuse all other Sudanese of impiety and of heresy, maintaining that only by force of arms can they be brought to repentance . . . They claim that they have undermined the foundations of religion by proclaiming illegal and criminal innovations to be legitimate, by shameful customs such as adultery, the use of fermented drinks, passion for amusement, song and dance, neglect of daily prayers, and refusal to offer alms for the poor. Each of these crimes and shameful deeds deserves vengeance and calls for a *jihad*. These ideas kindled the minds of the Fula for years, until suddenly there arose among them one renowned for his piety and godliness; the lion who became a reformer and proclaimed the holy war.

The lion was Uthman dan Fodio. Born a member of the Torodbe in 1754 in Gobir, the most northern of the Hausa states, he was well known even in his youth for his learning and religious zeal. He accepted a post as tutor to the court of Gobir and this gave him enough influence to be able to spread his ideas. By the 1780s his fame had led to the growth of a special community dedicated to his teaching and he was attracting a large number of pupils.

At first the local Hausa authorities were in two minds about this new development. In one sense, the presence of so important a man increased the prestige of Gobir, but, from another point of view, Uthman threatened their very existence and way of life. The fact was that his message went far beyond the narrowly religious. Quoting the Koran, he protested against illegal and oppressive taxes, attacked local customs, and insisted that the state should be governed according to strict Islamic law. This was a direct challenge to the relaxed governments of Gobir and the rest of Hausaland.

Over the years the relations between the various rulers of the Hausa states and the embarrassing religious community in their midst became increasingly strained. In 1796 the ruler of Gobir decided that he must try to limit the influence of Uthman and his followers. Strict orders were issued that anyone not born a Muslim should renounce the Islamic faith. This was specifically aimed at the Fula groups who had been converted from paganism by the new teaching. At the same time an attempt was made to destroy the separate identity of the new community by making it illegal for men to wear turbans and women veils, both distinguishing features of Uthman's followers. The ruler of Gobir was no more successful than Canute when he tried to halt the waves. It proved impossible to squash a genuine religious movement like Uthman's by administrative decree.

The exact moment when Uthman dan Fodio decided on a *jihad* is uncertain. He was certainly well acquainted with the circumstances that had led to Fula *jihads* during the eighteenth century in Futa Toro, Futa Jalon, and Masina. But what seems finally to have settled the matter was the hostile attitude of Yunfa who became ruler of Gobir in 1802. A former pupil of Uthman, Yunfa showed scant affection for his old teacher, who was forced to flee with many of his followers to the village where he had been born. There Yunfa attacked him and Uthman fled to Gudu which became the rallying-point for his followers, who quickly turned themselves into a large and formidable army.

The flight to Gudu was full of significance for those who accepted Uthman's teaching since it emphasized the parallel with the famous *hijra*, the flight of the Prophet from Mecca. Uthman was acclaimed Commander of the Faithful and he then declared a *jihad*. In doing so, he was careful to emphasize his exact intentions to his army and followers since he realized that there were many who had joined him for reasons that were very far from religious. 'If I fight this battle that I may become greater than my fellow,' he told them, 'or that my son may become greater than his son, or that my slave may lord it over his slave, may the infidel wipe us from the land.'

Uthman dan Fodio was not a military commander. He appointed his own generals, all except one being Fula, and himself gave advice about how the *jihad* should be conducted and the conquered territories administered. He laid down five principles of good government:

> The first is that authority shall not be given to one who seeks it. The second is the necessity for consultation. The third is the abandoning of harshness. The fourth is justice. The fifth is good works. And as for its ministers, they are four. The first is a trustworthy wazir to wake the ruler if he sleeps, to make him see if he is blind, and to remind him if he forgets, and the greatest misfortune for the government and the subjects is that they should be denied honest wazirs. And among the conditions pertaining to the wazir is that he should be steadfast in compassion to the people, and merciful towards them. The second of

10 The magnificent bodyguard of a Fula emir

the ministers is a judge whom the blame of a blamer cannot overtake concerning the affairs of God. The third is a chief of police who shall obtain justice for the weak from the strong. The fourth is a tax-collector who shall discharge his duties and not oppress the people . . .

The progress of the Fula armies through Hausaland was methodical and thorough. Katsina fell in 1807, Yunfa of Gobir was defeated and killed in

1808, and Kano was taken the following year. To the east, the ruler of Adamawa threw in his lot with the invaders and added another state to Uthman's empire. The *jihad* was also pushed southwards into the non-Sudanic area of the Niger. Nupe and Ilorin, the northern parts of the Oyo empire, fell to the Fula cavalry and became the main bases for Islamic attempts to penetrate into the thick forest of the Niger.

Only Bornu successfully resisted the Fula advance. Its survival was almost entirely due to the vigorous defence of Muhammad al-Kanemi, a warrior-scholar from east of Lake Chad. Al-Kanemi carried on an interesting war of words with Muhammad Bello, Uthman's favourite son, which sheds some light on the nature of the Fula *jihad* during its later stages. Basically he wanted to know what the war was about and why the Fula were bothering to attack an Islamic state like Bornu. Muhammad Bello set out a number of reasons all of which al-Kanemi, a notable and subtle scholar, was able to refute. The Fula leader then replied that since Bornu had assisted some of the Hausa rulers against the *jihad* it had consequently

11 Having surrendered much of his authority to al-Kanemi, the *mai* of Bornu holds an audience from the shelter of a bamboo cage

24

placed itself outside the 'Abode of Islam'. At this stage al-Kanemi wisely abandoned the inconclusive theological debate and concentrated on beating his enemy in battle. One result of his victory was that he became virtual ruler of Bornu, the *mais* being reduced to a mere puppet figure. Hugh Clapperton, the Scottish explorer who visited Bornu in 1821, felt some sympathy for the old ruling House.

> The Sultanship of Bornu is but a name; the court still keeps up considerable state . . . this is the only privilege left them. When the sultan gives audience to strangers, he sits in a kind of cage, made of bamboo, through the bars of which he looks on his visitors . . .

The failure to defeat Bornu really marked the end of the Fula *jihad* and Uthman dan Fodio retired to his books and his scholarship. Until his death in 1817 he remained the greatest figure in Hausaland, constantly urging the new Fula rulers to govern according to his own interpretation of Islamic law. He divided the empire into two but his son, Muhammad Bello, ruling from the new city of Sokoto, soon exerted the greater authority. A contemporary, Al Hajji Sa'id, wrote that under his rule

> The Hausa country flourished . . . He was sympathetic to the people and full of care for them, calm, patient, indifferent to the wealth of other men. A skilful administrator, he watched over the work of his officials, quashed judgements if these had been given under the influence of passion, never allowing them to grow slack in their work . . .

By the 1840s the main impetus of the *jihad* was spent. Nevertheless, its effects remained great. Hausaland was now almost totally Muslim both in the cities and the rural areas. The new Fula rulers made a sincere attempt to rule according to Islamic law and, although old abuses crept back, there was probably more security and justice than under the previous régime. This was reflected in the continued manufacturing and trading successes of the region. The commercial activity of Kano made a lasting impression on the German explorer, Heinrich Barth, when he visited it in 1851.

> In fact, if we consider that this industry is not carried on here as in Europe, in immense establishments, degrading men to the meanest condition of life, but that it gives employment and support to families without compelling them to sacrifice their domestic habits, we must presume that Kano ought to be one of the happiest countries in the world . . .

25

12   A late nineteenth-century print of Admadu's palace at Segu.
The man smoking suggests a laxity that Ahmadu would hardly have tolerated

'Happy' is probably not the word that would be used to describe the plight of the local inhabitants after two further *jihads* further north that were inspired by Uthman dan Fodio's example. In 1810 Ahmadu bin Hammadi Boubou, a Fula cleric who had studied under Uthman, returned to his home in Masina. In 1818 he proclaimed a *jihad* and by 1827 had extended his rule from Masina as far as Upper Volta and Timbuktu. Ahmadu's rule and that of his successors may have been efficient but there was no room for compromise as far as religion was concerned. There was as a result a constant undercurrent of unrest among the unhappy subjects against this fierce theocratic system. Barth disliked what he saw of it at Timbuktu, claiming that the new rulers were 'far more fanatical of the faith than the Arabs and Moors' and that they treated everyone 'with extreme rigour, according to the prejudices which they had imbibed'.

It was not surprising, therefore, that the invasion of Masina in 1862–63 by Al-Hajj Umar was welcomed, but the consequences for the unfortunate inhabitants were if anything worse. In 1826 Umar left Futa Toro for a pilgrimage to Mecca. There he became a member of the Tijaniyya brotherhood, a community that, like the sixteenth-century Calvinists in Europe,

26

13   For centuries a centre of trade and learning, Timbuktu remained a prize worth taking, forming the eastern limit of Umar's empire

believed that God had specially chosen them for salvation. Consequently, they regarded themselves as superior to all other Muslims whom they despised almost as much as they did pagans. The 'Abode of Islam' was for them a very small place indeed.

On his journey home from Mecca, Umar sampled the different forms of Islam that the western Sudan could provide. He went to al-Kanemi's Bornu, visited Sokoto where he married one of Muhammad Bello's daughters, and then went to the Masina of Ahmadu. The result of this particular pilgrim's progress was to make this zealous Tijani into the most uncompromising of the *jihad* leaders. Unlike the others, he equipped his armies with European rifles bought on the coast and quickly conquered Segu and Kaarta. Ahmadu III of Masina tried to delay Umar's advance by conducting a paper war in the style of al-Kanemi's with Muhammad Bello. The arguments and the results were equally inconclusive. By 1863 Masina had fallen and Umar's empire had reached Timbuktu.

Umar himself was killed in a rising during the following year and it was significant that it took his son ten years to establish his own authority. The fact was that Umar's particular brand of Islam was far too extreme for many like the Fula of Masina who considered themselves perfectly respectable Muslims already. Not surprisingly, therefore, the empire of Umar and his successors was a fragile affair compared with Hausaland under the Fula emirs. There were frequent insurrections, while its western border was threatened towards the end of the century not only by the French but by Samori, a Mande-speaking warlord from Guinea who tried to stem the European advance and nibble away at Umar's empire. Only the French were successful in the complicated struggle and by 1900 they had taken control of most of the area.

The *jihads* had created a series of remarkable theocratic states, the main legacy of which was the continued strength of Islam and its institutions throughout large parts of West Africa. It was perhaps fitting that Uthman dan Fodio's own creation in Hausaland should have lasted the longest. When it was eventually absorbed into Nigeria by the British towards the end of the scramble, the new administrators were sufficiently impressed by Fula rule to allow it to continue. This system of 'indirect rule' as it was called had its faults and its critics. But it enabled the framework of Fula rule to withstand the pressures of independence for Nigeria in 1963. Significantly, the great Fula leader, Sir Ahmadu Bello, the sultan of Sokoto, became the first prime minister of the new Nigeria. It was a final tribute to Uthman dan Fodio, the ideals of the *jihads*, and the great reformation of Islam in western Africa during the nineteenth century.

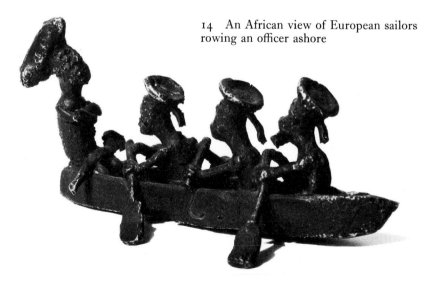

14   An African view of European sailors rowing an officer ashore

2 West Africa

SEPARATING THE SUDANIC states from the West African coast is an area which is very different geographically from the northern grasslands. Stretching from the Cameroon mountains in the east to the Gambia river in the west is an almost continuous belt of forest. In places this forest creeps down to the sea itself where it joins the harbourless beaches of the Gold and Ivory coasts and the tangled mangroves that lead into the Niger delta.

Because of its hazards to health, the whole area has always had an unfortunate reputation among outsiders. This was the region of 'the white man's grave' though it proved equally inhospitable to the Sudanic peoples. The main causes of these difficulties were the malaria-carrying mosquito and the tsetse-fly which caused sleeping sickness and was fatal to hooved animals. Not until after 1850 did Europeans discover that quinine gave them a large degree of immunity to these diseases.

The whole of this forest was fairly densely populated and there had grown up there a number of notable political systems. In 1800 the most important were the old empires of Benin and Oyo and the more recent ones of Ashanti and Dahomey. Further, scattered among the complicated delta area of the Niger were some smaller but far from insignificant trading states, offering the best ports along the whole West African coast.

The Forest States and the North

It might have been expected that the close proximity of the Islamic *jihads* would have affected some of these forest states. But, apart from the Fula invasion of the northern parts of the Yoruba empire of Oyo, the Islamic revival had only a limited influence. One reason for this was the very real strength of traditional West African paganism. Another was the inability of the northern cavalry to penetrate far into the forest because of the tsetse-fly.

29

Nevertheless, there were important contacts between the Sudanic peoples and those of the forest. Perhaps symbolic of this was the veneration shown in Benin towards the horse in an area which could not have been more unsuitable for cavalry. More significant was the existence in nearly all the forest states of comparatively large urban centres similar to those of the north. Ancient Benin, for example, seems to have been sufficiently grand to impress a Dutch visitor as early as 1602.

> The town seems to be very great; when you enter it, you go into a great broad street . . . which seems to be seven or eight times broader than Warmors street in Amsterdam . . . The houses in this town stand in good order, one close and even with the other, as the houses in Holland stand.

The main channel of influence between the forest states and the north was trade. The chief forest commodities were gold-dust, some ivory, and

15 A fine example of Benin ivory carving. The suggestion of Portuguese influence in the headdress indicates contact through the slave trade

16   A print of 1832 showing slaves on the way
to the coast. There is little attempt to depict
the agonies involved in such journeys

kola nuts, used to make a drink which was the nearest the Muslims were
allowed to an alcoholic beverage. In its turn, the south received cloth,
beads, and other trans-Saharan goods. As this trade developed, West African slaves were included and they continued to be sent north until well
after 1800.

These commercial links flourished in spite of real practical limits on
movement imposed by the forest. The tsetse-fly made it impossible to use
beasts of burden so that, apart from the rivers, the only form of transport
was that of slave labour. Sir James Stephen, the conscientious British civil
servant at the old Colonial Department, used to be thoroughly upset by
officials on the spot who condoned this form of domestic slavery. Only
grudgingly did he come to admit that such slaves played a necessary part in
the economic life of West Africa.

The Transatlantic Slave Trade

Stephen was particularly concerned about the whole distasteful business of
the transatlantic slave trade. But in confusing domestic slavery and the

slave trade, he was dimly aware that the two went together in origin. Local African rulers had been quick to develop the trade from their own native system once there was a serious demand for slaves, first from the north and then in larger numbers from the coast.

The transatlantic slave trade was the first major contact between West Africans and Europeans. It is impossible to estimate exactly how many slaves were taken from West Africa during the 350 or so years of its existence. It was probably somewhere in the region of 10 million, but such a figure cannot include those who died in the course of capture or during the miseries of 'the middle passage' on board ship. The trade was by far the most important influence on West African history before the colonial period. It introduced fear and misery among many people and by bringing in cheap European goods led to a decline in ancient skills and crafts. But no West African ruler could afford to ignore the trade and the firearms traffic that went with it. To do so might mean defeat, absorption, and for many an unwanted journey across the Atlantic at the hands of more realistic neighbours and their slave-trading associates.

It would be unjust to the already complex developments of these forest states to say that they owed their existence to the slave trade. Benin and Oyo, for example, were already strong before it began. But the trade certainly conditioned their future from the seventeenth century onwards as they quickly adapted themselves to the new commercial possibilities presented by the Europeans. The trade was normally conducted by a small number of Africans who acted as contractors under the direct control of the rulers who, as a consequence, were able to draw a substantial revenue from the sale of slaves. The result was that by the eighteenth century practically the whole state structure was geared to the slave trade.

In these circumstances, Britain's initiative during the nineteenth century in seeking an end to the trade had serious effects. Destruction did not come immediately since few other European nations or the United States fully shared Britain's sudden change of heart. To Sir Thomas Buxton, a leading British anti-slaver, the object was simply 'the deliverance of Africa, by calling forth her own resources'. But this emphasis on goods other than slaves sounded hollow and at times hypocritical when repeated in Paris, Lisbon, Rio de Janeiro, and Washington. It suggested that the Britain of the Industrial Revolution wanted to develop and even monopolize the legitimate trade of West Africa to the advantage of her own merchants and manufacturers.

Between 1825 and 1865 some 130,000 West African slaves were released largely through the work of the Royal Navy's West Africa Squadron. But in the same period substantially well over 1 million slaves were taken across the Atlantic. It was not until Brazil and the United States abolished slavery during the second half of the century that the trade eventually ground to a halt. One reason why it took so long to die was noticed as early as 1816 by a British naval officer:

Neither mountains, rivers nor deserts will prove barriers to the slave trade, as the black chiefs will bring their slaves from every extremity of Africa as long as there is a nation that will afford them a slave market.

MAP NO. 2
West Africa, eastern half, 1800–75

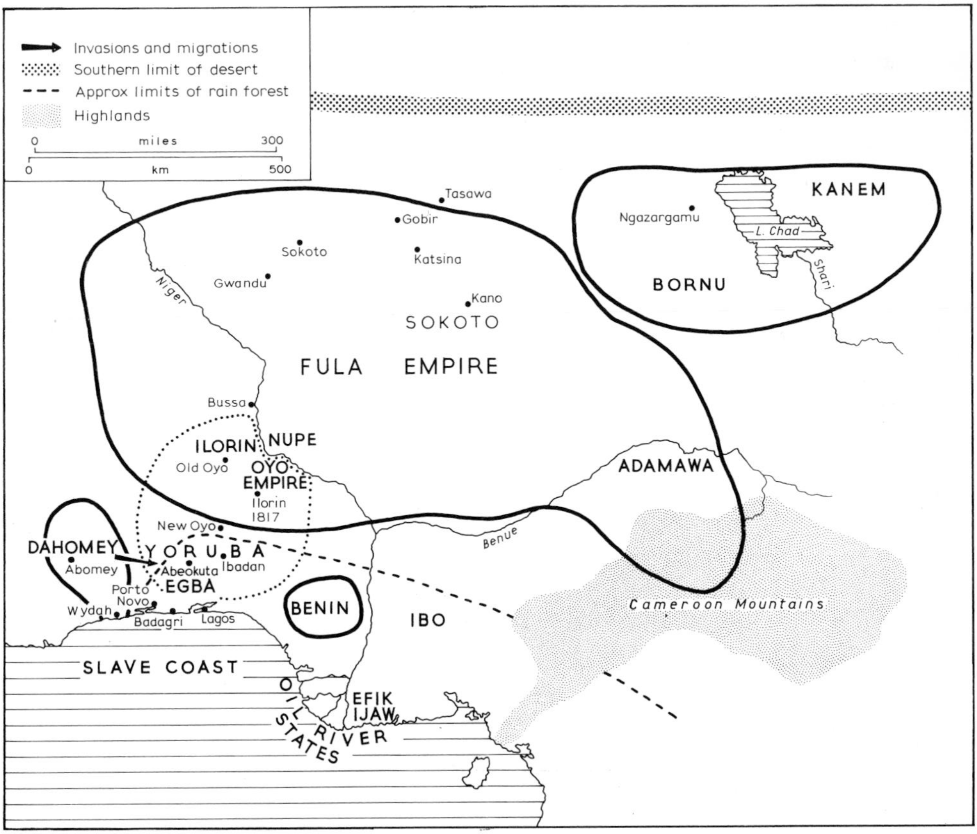

Legend:
→ Invasions and migrations
Southern limit of desert
- - - Approx limits of rain forest
Highlands

0 miles 300
0 km 500

Tasawa
Gobir
Sokoto
Katsina
Gwandu
Kano
Ngazargamu
KANEM
L. Chad
Shari
BORNU
SOKOTO
FULA EMPIRE
Niger
Bussa
ILORIN NUPE
Old Oyo
OYO EMPIRE
Ilorin 1817
ADAMAWA
New Oyo
Benue
DAHOMEY YORUBA
Abomey Abeokuta Ibadan
Porto EGBA
Novo
Wydah
Badagri Lagos
BENIN
IBO
Cameroon Mountains
SLAVE COAST
OIL RIVER STATES
EFIK IJAW

17 Slaves were kept in huts, or baracoons, until a
slave ship arrived. During the 1840s the British
navy destroyed these bases, until one slaver sued
for loss of property

The trade had by this time become too ingrained an institution in African
society to be abandoned easily. Rarely, for example, was there any confidence on either side over the anti-slave-trade treaties between Britain and
the African rulers. King Pepple of Bonny once told a European merchant,
'one white man come and make book [treaty] and another white man come
tomorrow and break it. White man be fool, best treaty is in my head.'

Most African rulers were unconvinced by the arguments of British
humanitarians that legitimate commerce would bring them greater benefits
than the slave trade. Nevertheless, the attack on the trade had serious
consequences. By first of all introducing a note of uncertainty and then by
gradually closing the most lucrative markets, the anti-slave-trade interests
began to undermine the economic foundations of the West African states.
This in its turn meant a loss of revenue to their rulers which, coming at
a time when many faced serious problems in other directions, finally
weakened their authority and contributed to their final collapse.

18 The practice of burning the baracoons was
renewed in the late 1840s, as this scene off
the Solyman river in 1849 shows

The Oil River States

The most easily exploitable legitimate products of the area were palm oil,
used in Europe for soap, candles, and lubricants, and palm kernels which
after the 1870s became the basis of the margarine industry. British hopes
that these goods might be developed to the point where they would force a
complete end to the slave trade were encouraged by events along the Niger
delta.

The delta area had never been controlled by any one ruler but, under the
stimulus of the slave trade, a number of vigorous trading states had
emerged. The most important of these were Bonny, New Calabar, Brass,
and Okrika among the Ijo people and the Efik state of Old Calabar. Most of
them possessed kings but the real centre of power lay with the 'house',
trading associations of freemen and slaves headed by a chief. Not only were
they the main channels of commerce but these 'houses' also played a vital

role in their communities politically and socially. Some were sufficiently flexible to allow a slave to become head of his particular 'house'. Such a one was Ja Ja who, after taking over one of the Bonny 'houses', then established his own city-state at Opobo in 1870. He soon had an almost complete monopoly of the delta palm oil trade. His acute business sense as well as his considerable political power so infuriated the British that in 1887 they arrested him and deported him to the West Indies.

In the hey-day of the slave trade, the delta states had drawn most of their slaves from the Ibos of the immediate hinterland. The Ibos lived in towns and villages which consisted largely of extended family groups. They were bound together by common cultural and religious ties and by their genius as traders. The nearest there was to any kind of central Ibo institution was the influential oracle of Aro Chuku. Its main source of wealth was the control it established over the slave trade by a combination of military threats and religious terror. Although its power declined as the palm oil

19 Ja Ja was perhaps the most famous of a number of enterprising slaves who used the fluid social system of the Oil River States to become an important palm oil merchant

20 King Pepple of Bonny, whose capital was a flourishing trading centre, was a considerable thorn in the flesh of the British, who deposed him in 1854

trade grew, it was still important when the British explorer, W. B. Baikie, visited the Ibo region in 1854. He arrived at

the noted city of Aro where there is the celebrated shrine of Tshuku (God), to which pilgrimages are made, not only from all parts of Igbo proper, but from Old Calabar and the tribes along the coast . . . The town is always mentioned with great respect, almost, at times, with a degree of veneration, and the people say 'Tshuku ab yama' or 'God lives there.'

During the 1830s and 1840s the Liverpool merchants began to develop the palm oil trade fairly intensively using the existing institutions of the delta states. With extraordinary adaptability these states and the Ibos inland adjusted themselves to the new situation. For some forty years they controlled the trade with skill and tenacity and normally on their own terms. There were, of course, disagreements between the Africans and the Europeans. In the late 1840s the British appointed consuls to what they now called the 'Oil Rivers' in an attempt to iron out these difficulties. Not unnaturally this led to increasing British interference in the political as well as the economic life of the delta states, particularly in the affairs of Bonny.

37

In 1855 the British presence was only too obviously felt when Old Calabar was destroyed by naval bombardment.

Perhaps the most significant date was 1854 when Baikie took a ship up the Niger and, because he was using quinine, returned without any loss of life to Europeans. The possibility of direct British trading in the hinterland became as a result far more real and the days of the delta middlemen were numbered. At first the Liverpool merchants discouraged this kind of active penetration since it threatened their careful arrangements with the delta states. But once the scramble began and, more particularly, as Ja Ja threatened their interests, they revised their opinions. In 1885 Britain set up the Oil Rivers Protectorate and the economic independence of the delta states and the Ibos had come to an end.

The Forest States: Ashanti and Dahomey

In the forest itself, the empire-states of Ashanti, Dahomey, Benin, and Oyo, all at some time involved in the slave trade, were distinguished from the delta states by their greater size and the strength of their armies. Of these, Ashanti and Dahomey remained the most vigorous until the 1890s, displaying considerable diplomatic and military skill in defence of their independence.

The quarrels of the Ashanti and their southern neighbours the Fante dominated the Gold Coast for most of the nineteenth century. Both groups stemmed from the Akan peoples who had moved into the region during the twelfth and thirteenth centuries. The Ashanti had settled in that part of the forest where the trade routes from Timbuktu and Hausaland joined and where the main deposits of gold were to be found. Until well into the nineteenth century they continued to trade with the north where for a time a number of minor Islamic states were part of their empire.

The foundations of Ashanti strength were laid by Osei Tutu (c. 1697–c. 1731). According to tradition, his priest, Anokye, in the presence of the neighbouring chiefs, caused a golden stool to descend from the sky on to the king's knees. This stool was accepted as representing the united spirit of the Ashanti. This powerful symbol introduced into the new Ashanti union a dual loyalty, one to the local chief, the other to the *asantehene*, the ruler at the capital at Kumasi and the guardian of the golden stool. By 1800 this union was large and powerful. The first British mission reached

Kumasi in 1817 and one of its members, T. E. Bowdich, wrote:

> Our observations *en passant* had taught us to conceive a spectacle far exceeding our original expectations; but they had not prepared us for the extent and display of the scene which had burst upon us; an area of nearly a mile in circumference was crowded with magnificence and novelty. The king, his tributaries, and captains, were resplendent in the distance, surrounded by attendants of every description, fronted by a mass of warriors . . . The sun was reflected, with a glare scarcely more supportable than the heat, from the massive gold ornaments which glistened in every direction. More than a hundred bands burst at once on our arrival . . .

Bowdich was particularly complimentary about the *asantehene*, considering his views 'incredibly liberal . . . they seemed to break the spell which has shut the interior'.

When Bowdich talked about the interior being shut, he put his finger on the key to Ashanti history during the nineteenth century. Their early expansion had given them a monopoly of the slave and gold trades of the interior but what they wanted was to end the control of the mainly Fante middlemen between them and the coast so that they could trade directly with the Europeans. Since the Fante had no particular desire to allow this,

21 A view of a courtyard at Kumasi, from Bowdich's account of his travels

22 A drawing dating from the British
campaign against the Ashanti (1873–74)

war was the only possible solution. The first had occurred as early as 1765 and there were nine more during the nineteenth century.

The whole situation was highly complex and full of paradox. The Fante, far from united, needed the assistance of Europeans, mainly the British, to defend a commercial system now well over a hundred years old. The Ashanti on their side were anxious for direct relations with the Europeans but to obtain it had to fight among others the British. That they were acutely aware of the changing nature of European trade was made clear to the 1817 mission by the *asantehene* when he 'scowled with indignation at the statement . . . that Europeans considered that he made war for the purpose of procuring slaves'. But Ashanti willingness to engage in legitimate trade was made more difficult in a region where, according to Sir James Stephen, the products were 'of less value to us . . . than the trade with the Isle of Skye'.

In this confused situation, the Ashanti armies were normally victorious but they were never quite strong enough ever completely to dominate the coast. The unfortunate Fante states were not helped by the total inability

depicting them in a sinister light. Note the
stool, symbol of the *asantehene*'s authority

of the British to make up their minds about the future of their precarious
trading stations on the Gold Coast. George Maclean, a young army officer
sent out as president of the Council of Merchants, at least tried to lay down
some firm guide lines for the future. An essentially pragmatic man, respected by all the chiefs of the area, he managed to guarantee the Ashanti open
access to the sea by a treaty in 1831. In order to assure this freedom of trade
he began to exercise an unofficial form of jurisdiction over the Fante
leaders which most of them were prepared to accept. There was an immediate increase in legitimate commerce but still the London authorities remained afraid about committing themselves in the Gold Coast area. Although Maclean's work was legalized by the 1844 Bonds with the Fante,
few of his successors shared his understanding of the main problems. Trade
began to decline again and in 1865 a Select Committee of the Commons
suggested that Britain should cut its losses in West Africa except in Sierra
Leone which had been founded in 1781 as a home for freed slaves.

Faced with such indications of British hesitation, the Fante tried to
organize themselves. In 1871 a group of educated Africans and chiefs

meeting at Mankessim drew up the first modern African constitution which would have created a federation headed by a president with an executive council and an elected assembly. Given the vacillations of British policy, those responsible for the plan were surprised to find themselves promptly arrested for conspiracy.

Under these circumstances and with the 1831 Treaty increasingly a dead letter, the Ashanti turned the trade routes once more into war paths. But at this juncture (1873–74) the British sent Sir Garnet Wolseley and a force of regular troops to Kumasi. The Ashanti capital was captured and burned after a hard campaign. There was no intention at that time of annexing Ashanti, which prompted one critic to say that Wolseley ran 'into Kumasi and out again like a ferret in a rabbit-hole'. There were, in fact, to be further Ashanti campaigns before the area was declared a Crown Colony in 1902. The period of colonial rule did little to mend the divisions between Ashanti and Fante, the product of over a century of confusion and warfare. If anything they were made worse since the Fante, with their longer contacts with the British, adjusted themselves far more quickly to European ideas and values. It was educated Africans of the Fante area who led the campaign for independence in the years after 1945 while the Ashanti looked on with fear and suspicion.

To the east, the limits of Ashanti expansion were set by the powerful state of Dahomey. Emerging in the seventeenth century, it was for a time part of the western fringe of the Yoruba empire of Oyo, but by 1800 it had become independent. Unlike Ashanti, Dahomey had direct access to the sea at Wydah and indulged in the slave trade in return for firearms as long as slavers were prepared to visit the coast. In 1772, one of them, Robert Norris, went to Abomey, the capital. On each side of the entrance to the palace he was horrified to find

> a human head, recently cut off, lying on a flat stone ... In the guard house were about forty women, armed with a musket and a cutlass each ... We passed through a third door into the court where the king was seated ... He was smoking tobacco ... Several women were employed fanning him, and others with whisks to chase away the flies; one woman, on her knees before him, held a gold cup for him to spit in.

Throughout the nineteenth century European visitors to Abomey were discouraged, but those who managed to get there were always received with similar intimidating displays.

42

23   Gezo, king of Dahomey. This print reflects the effectiveness of Dahomeian
efforts to convince the outside world of their calculated cruelty

But accounts of large-scale human sacrifice and fierce female guards may
well have been deliberately encouraged by Dahomey to dissuade Europeans from coming. It was not without significance that the capital was far
inland and that by tradition the king must never look upon the sea. Any
visiting mission then had a long and often uncongenial journey before it
could conduct its business. Kings Gezo (1818–58) and Gelele (1858–89)
were masters at combining sinister traditional methods with acute diplomacy in their attempts to avoid conflict with Europeans.

Sir Richard Burton, British explorer and, for a time during the early
1860s, consul at Fernando Po, argued that Dahomey would 'crumble to
pieces with the first heavy shock'. Gezo and Gelele might secretly have
agreed with this analysis. The British blockade was already underlining that

43

24   Cape Coast Castle, once a slave-trading fort. In the 1830s Maclean tried from here to mediate between the Ashanti and Fante

the slave trade could only be carried on in the future with difficulty. More serious was Dahomey's failure in the 1850s and 1860s to take advantage on its eastern border of the Yoruba civil wars, a fruitful source of slaves. Nevertheless, the British official, B. C. Cruickshank, was less than just to the policies of Dahomey when he concluded his report on a visit there in 1848 by arguing that Britain might as soon 'expect the confirmed gambler, sharper, or black-leg to earn his livelihood by patient and honest industry, as to see a slave-dealing king and people become suddenly painstaking agriculturists.' For, unlike some other West African rulers, those in Dahomey reacted to the changing patterns of trade with sense and imagination. In 1841 a Marseilles firm began trading at Wydah in palm oil. Both Gezo and Gelele were anxious to keep this new trade as far as possible in royal hands. A good deal of it was conducted outside the monarchy's control by individuals working in the forest, but Gezo increased his revenue by establishing slave-worked plantations. It is true that a substantial amount of the profit was used to acquire firearms since slaving still continued as long as there were buyers. Nevertheless, the export of palm oil products from Dahomey was worth almost £½ million by the 1870s. But with the growth of this new trade came increasing French interest in the area. Gezo and Gelele had managed to survive most of the century without firing a shot against any European. It was unfortunate that in 1892 one was aimed at a French official. It was the signal for the annexation of Dahomey although in places resistance to alien rule continued until as late as 1911.

44

The Forest States: Benin and Oyo

The two older forest states, Benin and Oyo, had by 1800 lost much of their earlier vigour compared with Ashanti and Dahomey. Both of them traditionally had their origins in the old settlement of Ife and inherited from there a sensitivity in sculpture and metal-working that was far in advance of other parts of tropical Africa. Both states had been involved in the slave trade, particularly Oyo, but in the changing conditions of the nineteenth century they found it difficult to adjust to the new situation.

25 A nineteenth-century Yoruba wood-carving of an officer standing to attention

26 A carved figure of an *Oni* in the traditional robes used at coronation ceremonies in Ife, Western Nigeria

The position of Benin was in many ways odd and difficult to assess. It appeared to be the least able to change and at the same time found it the easiest to survive. Its empire had been at its strongest during the sixteenth and seventeenth centuries but even then it had been a fairly loose structure dependent on the character and personality of the *oba* at Benin. Traditionally, the explanation for Benin's collapse during the nineteenth century has been seen largely in economic terms. The *oba's* control over the slave trade had been weakened by years of depopulating raids and by the success of the tributary chiefs in diverting the trade into their own hands. This particular argument, however, underestimates the political tensions within the Benin empire and especially the desire of the vassal states to be independent of the *oba's* control. There is some evidence to suggest that Benin had never been a great slaving state and that the trade had always been primarily concentrated in the hands of the tributary chiefs. If this was the case it would only strengthen the argument that they deliberately tried to cut off Benin proper from the outside world in an attempt to increase their own freedom of action. The result seems to be that Benin survived most of the nineteenth century in isolation, consumed with its own internal quarrels over the succession and consequently gaining neither the respect nor the tribute of the vassal states. This was certainly Burton's impression in 1862. He was told by the Itsekiri that 'when he is strong, the people pay him the customs of olden times; when he is weak, they laugh at his beard'.

During most of the nineteenth century then Benin was little more than an inept rump of a once-great empire doing little harm to anyone but itself and totally incapable of exerting its authority over its former vassals. During the latter part of the scramble the then *oba* bungled some negotiations with the British and a punitive expedition was sent in 1897. Its commander, R. H. Bacon, was upset by the conditions he found in Benin. 'Crucifixions, human sacrifices, and every horror the eye could get accustomed to, to a large extent, but the smells no white man's internal economy could stand.' The British decided in the next year 'to do away with a reign of terror and all its accompanying horrors'. It was a sad epitaph on one of the oldest and most cultivated African empires.

The collapse of the Yoruba empire of Oyo was, however, of far greater significance. By plunging the Yorubas into a series of bitter civil wars, the weakening of Oyo's authority attracted the attention of the slavers because of the abnormally large number of captives offered for sale. Automatically Britain's anti-slave-trade efforts were concentrated on the area and as the

46

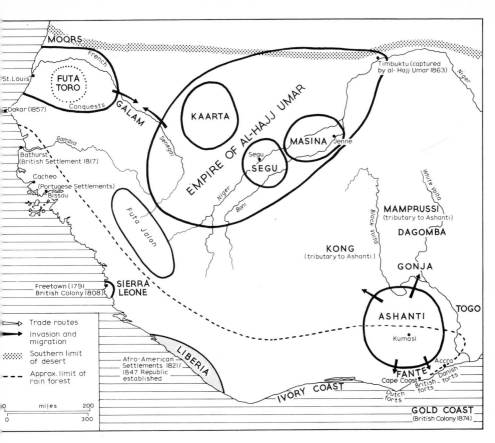

MAP NO. 3
West Africa, western half, 1800-75

century progressed they became increasingly involved in Yoruba affairs.

Oyo's expansion had begun in the seventeenth century. Its centre lay to the north of the forest and its authority was acknowledged by Borgu and Nupe towards the southern extremities of Hausaland. Drawn southwards by the slave trade, Oyo extended its power to the coast during the eighteenth century, pulling into its orbit a number of smaller forest states. By 1800 it was a state that gave the impression of great strength and prosperity. A nineteenth-century sea captain claimed that its cloth was superior 'both for variety of pattern, colour and dimensions, to any made in the

47

neighbouring states' while the Sierra Leone priest and historian Samuel Johnson, could still discern the fine qualities of its peoples at a time when the old order of Oyo had collapsed.

> The ancient Oyos or Yorubas ... were very virtuous, loving and kind ... Now they are remarkably patient of injuries ... They are characteristically unassuming in their manners and submissive to their superiors.

But increasingly weaknesses were becoming evident that were in the 1820s and 1830s to destroy the Oyo empire. Its size and complexity demanded of its rulers, the *alafins*, a degree of control that Yoruba tradition rarely was able to tolerate. If the leader of the council announced to the *alafin* that 'the gods reject you, the people reject you, the earth rejects you', he had no choice but to commit suicide. Inevitably, therefore, there was tension between the need for strong rule and the considerable limitations placed on his authority. This particular constitutional weakness was aggravated at the end of the eighteenth century by a zealous leader of the royal council who engineered the murder of a succession of rulers. This was the tragic prologue to a series of crises that were to tear Oyo apart.

The problems at the centre were reflected in the increasing unrest among Oyo's subject states who saw the opportunity to establish their own political autonomy. Closely connected with this was their anxiety to retain the profits of the slave trade without reference to Oyo. By 1800 Dahomey and the Egba, in the south of the empire, had established their independence. Nearer the capital a confused situation developed from 1817 onwards involving Oyo's immediate neighbour, Ilorin, and invading Fula armies from the north. The ruler of Ilorin sent the *alafin*, Aole, an empty calabash indicating that he no longer accepted his authority. Before killing himself as tradition demanded, Aole, after shooting arrows to the north, south, and west, threatened his people:

> My curse be on you for your disloyalty and disobedience; so let your children disobey you. If you send them on an errand, let them never return to bring you word again. To all points I shot my arrows will you be carried as slaves. My curse will carry you to the sea and beyond, slaves will rule over you, and you, their masters will become slaves.

It turned out to be less a curse than an accurate prediction of what was to happen to the Yorubas in the immediate future.

When Ilorin invited the aid of the Fulas, it brought to the northern

27 A Yoruba chief wearing his ceremonial dress and mask

Yorubas the full force of the *jihad*. Ilorin itself became an Islamic emirate along with Nupe. The Fula advance was only halted between 1837 and 1840 by the difficulties of fighting in the forest and by the newly created city-state of Ibadan. In about 1835 Oyo itself was obliterated and the remnants of its inhabitants founded New Oyo 100 miles to the south.

The collapse in the north of the *alafin's* authority encouraged the southern Yorubas and others to form a number of new states of which Ibadan was one. Others included the Egba state of Abeokuta and the Ijebu states along the coastal lagoons. Only a part of their energy was spent in resisting the Fula and the slave raids of Dahomey. Many of them were engaged extensively in the slave trade which expanded rapidly during the 1830s and 1840s as civil wars and inter-state rivalry spread. Just as important was the need to fill the power vacuum left by the collapse of Oyo but since none of the southern Yoruba states was strong enough to establish complete ascendancy, the wars lasted for the rest of the century. This major crisis was highlighted by the serious tension between Ibadan and the Egba which, beginning in the 1860s, soon involved all the Yoruba peoples before Britain's final intervention during the scramble.

28 The disastrous consequences of the Yoruba
wars are clearly illustrated by this early photograph of a village, burned and destroyed

There were further complications that added bitterness to the Yoruba wars. As the slave trade declined and after the British took over complete control of Lagos in 1861, the demand for palm oil products began to increase. As in Dahomey, this posed a serious problem for the Yoruba rulers. Some of them, anxious to keep their own revenue as high as possible, tried to farm the palm oil themselves. This involved the use of slave labour so that paradoxically one result of the introduction of legitimate trade was to continue slave-raiding wars. This was certainly one element in the rivalry between the Yoruba states although it should not be exaggerated. But the rulers were rarely able to win a monopoly of the palm oil trade since they had to compete with the large number of small farmers capable of collecting the kernels themselves. This forced many of the rulers to prop up their sometimes precarious fortunes by engaging in warfare at their neighbour's expense. Samuel Johnson commented bitterly on the sad results in 1886:

> It is heart-rending to think of the effects of this unfortunate war. Many families have been ruined. There are instances of the father, the stay of the family, having died; one and another of his sons who succeeded him having also perished in the war, and the rest of the family scattered. Slaves who redeemed themselves were resold by their former masters; and many of the chiefs were compelled to part with their slave wives to procure arms and meet war expenses.

In the circumstances the British traders encouraged a forward policy to end what was fast becoming a chaotic situation among the Yorubas. During the 1890s the small Lagos protectorate was extended to include most of what had been the southern part of the empire of Oyo. Benin too was absorbed while the north was conquered by the troops of the Royal Niger Company. Together with the delta states and the Ibo territory they were all subsequently combined into the colony of Nigeria.

The African Agency

The nineteenth century saw the collapse of much of the political and economic framework of the West African states and the establishment towards its close of colonial rule. The colonial period, however, was to prove relatively short, some sixty or seventy years only. One reason for this was that even while so much of the old Africa was disintegrating, the means were

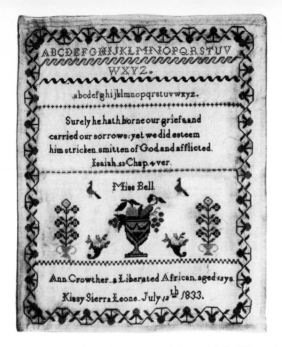

On the sampler:
ABCDEFGHIJKLMNOPQRSTUV
WXYZ.
abcdefghijklmnopqrstuvwxyz.

Surely he hath borne our grief and
carried our sorrows: yet we did esteem
him stricken, smitten of God and afflicted.
Isaiah 53 Chap. 4 ver.

Miss Bell

Ann Crowther a Liberated African aged 13ys.
Kissy Sierra Leone. July 13ᵗʰ 1833.

29 A sampler worked
by a liberated African
girl in Sierra Leone.
There is something
patronizing in a young
African being taught the
exact skills of her
contemporaries in Britain

already being created by which West Africa was to become independent
during the middle years of the twentieth century.

In 1846, a young Sierra Leone African, George Nicol, wrote before
going to England to train as an Anglican priest that

> I am deeply convinced . . . that if Africa could be raised from its present state
> of barbarism, superstition and vice . . . recourse must be had to the native
> agencies. Africans themselves must be the principal harbingers of peace.

This idea of the 'African agency' owed something to the thinking of Sir
Thomas Buxton and Henry Venn who became secretary to the Church
Missionary Society in 1841. In part they were reacting to the failure in that
year of Buxton's scheme to establish an experimental farm on the upper
reaches of the Niger. The death through disease of so many Europeans on
the expedition reinforced their view that Western-educated Africans, still
with some sympathy for their former tribal backgrounds, might be the best
agents for introducing Christianity and the simpler techniques of scientific
farming.

One particular African had also been convinced of the importance of
using Africans by his experiences on the Niger expedition. Samuel Ajayi
Crowther had been captured during the Yoruba wars and sold as a slave.
He was rescued by the Royal Navy and in Sierra Leone became one of the

first pupils of Fourah Bay College. He went as a linguist on the 1841 expedition and as a result of its disasters decided to become a missionary priest. His philosophy was simple but important.

> God had provided instruments to begin the work in the liberated Africans . . . It would be of very great advantage if the colony-born young men were introduced by their parents to their fatherland . . . They are brought back to their country as a renewed people, looked upon by their countrymen as superior to themselves, as long as they continue consistent in their Christian work and conversation.

Crowther first worked at Abeokuta and then he set up a chain of mission stations along the Niger, an extraordinary achievement given the unsettled conditions among the Yorubas. The significance of his work was recognized in 1864 when he was consecrated the first African bishop in the Anglican Church.

30   Bishop Crowther, anglicized and Anglican, who, nevertheless, did much to restore the self-respect of West Africans in both European eyes and their own

31 An ebony carving of an *oba* of Benin, a
kingdom that inherited much of the skill of the
Ife craftsmen

32 A carved figure of Queen Victoria,
by a Yoruba craftsman

There was a tendency for some of these men to underestimate the
achievements of African society and to emphasize unduly the worst aspects
of contemporary life. It was a reaction not dissimilar to that of many Europeans and it had the advantage of appealing to humanitarian sympathies in
Britain and elsewhere. Crowther himself reflected this kind of attitude and

54

remained throughout his life something of a grand Victorian figure. Others, like the Reverend Samuel Johnson, had a more sympathetic understanding of African culture and history. Such men, moving into their former homelands, represented a new focus of attention. In 1851 the small Christian mission at Abeokuta inspired the successful defence of the city against Dahomey. More significant, during the 1870s the educated élite there set up the Egba United Board of Management in an attempt to modernize the state and so prevent its probable absorption by Britain. This attempt to graft the ideas of the West on to the local African traditions was similar to the abortive experiment of the Mankessim constitution on the Gold Coast. What these men were trying to do may not have been very successful at first but the ultimate significance of their work was revolutionary. They saw European ideas as a means of regenerating African society but at the same time they never forgot that Africans deserved both trust and responsibility. It is one of the paradoxes of nineteenth-century African history that at a time when other parts of the continent were still largely unknown to Europeans, modern nationalism was already beginning to emerge in Sierra Leone, the Gold Coast, and along the banks of the Niger.

33   A group of European missionaries being
received at a Yoruba village in 1856

55

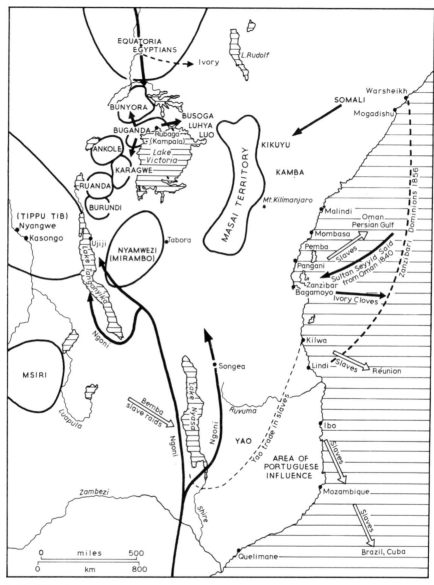

MAP NO. 4
East Central Africa, 1800–84

3. East Africa

BECAUSE OF ITS GEOGRAPHY, East Africa has always contained a complicated variety of peoples and cultures. The coastal strip was reasonably fertile and owing to the commercial activity across the Indian Ocean there has always been something of a cosmopolitan atmosphere. Not far inland begins the wide expanse of dry plain that stretches as far as Lakes Tanganyika and Victoria. Except for some isolated pockets such as the Kenya Highlands this is a harsh and difficult region. With a slight and unpredictable rainfall, its agricultural lands have always been poor and its population small and thinly scattered. Along its western edge there runs a wide corridor from Lake Tanganyika to north of Lake Victoria. This region, separating the East African plain from the equally inhospitable humid forests of the Congo, is one of the most fortunate in the continent. The land is highly fertile and it has always had a high density of population. In the past the original Bantus had been faced with a number of invasions by Nilotes and Nilo-Hamites from the north and together these races had developed a number of well-organized states, the most important by the early nineteenth century being Buganda, Bunyoro, and Ruanda.

The Arab Traders

The coast of East Africa has attracted merchants from the earliest times. There is evidence that the Romans sailed down it, while in the fifteenth century Chinese fleets called at irregular intervals. During the sixteenth and seventeenth centuries the Portuguese established a number of bases there as part of their eastern empire. But the most consistent traders, able to take full advantage of the seasonal monsoons across the Indian Ocean, came from Arabia and to a lesser extent from India.

The Arab traders settled in urban communities along the whole coast from Somalia to the Zambesi. With them came Islam but this was far from

34 Sir Richard Burton, an early European explorer
in East Africa, and subsequently a consul in West
Africa. He felt little affection for Africa or Africans,
comparing them unfavourably with the Islamic world

being the militant faith seen at the beginning of the nineteenth century in
the Sudan. Far more important was the social intermingling of the Arabs
and the Bantu which produced along the coast a distinctive culture, neither
fully Arab nor completely African. Its language, Swahili, basically Bantu
but drawing a large number of words from Arabic, came to be spoken over

a considerable area of East Africa. When Dr Ludwig Krapf, the German missionary, arrived at Mombasa in 1844, he realized the immediate necessity for mastering the language and began to compile the first Swahili grammar. It was not an easy task but clearly had its compensations. He wrote:

> With the aid of Arabic, I surmounted this hindrance by degrees; but I found in it peculiarities which at first gave me immense trouble, but which also were converted into a source of delight when I was at length able to cry 'Eureka'.

Initially, only a few of these Arab–Swahili traders penetrated far into the interior, where, until the second quarter of the nineteenth century, the major trade routes were dominated by the Africans themselves. By far the most important route was that running from the Lake Tanganyika area to Zanzibar. At its eastern end there were important branches northwards to Lake Victoria and south-west into Katanga. It was from the latter that copper was taken to a large part of East Africa, being especially valuable to the lake states for ceremonial ornaments. The staple exports to the coast were slaves and ivory, the demand for the second growing throughout the nineteenth century.

The route to Zanzibar was dominated by the Nyamwezi, a vigorous people living among fairly good farming land to the south of Lake Victoria. They ranged far and wide and Msiri, the last great ruler of Katanga, was a member of the tribe. Burton, travelling in the region in 1858, could not resist making some disparaging remarks about them.

> The Wanyamwezi have won for themselves a reputation by their commercial industry. Encouraged by the merchants [on the coast], they are the only professional porters of East Africa . . . They are no longer 'honest and civil to strangers' – semi-civilization has hitherto tended to degradation. They seem to have learned but little by their intercourse with the Arabs. Commerce with them is still in its infancy. They have no idea of credit, although . . . payment may be delayed for a period of two years.

Burton's sourness was no doubt sweetened by the fact that by the middle of the century this African control of the main trade routes was being challenged by the Arabs. The initiative in this came from Zanzibar whose ruler, Seyyid Said, also the sultan of Muscat and Oman in southern Arabia, was increasingly interested in his East African dominions. Omani influence dated back to the sixteenth and seventeenth centuries when successive sultans had driven the Portuguese off the coast except for the area of Mozambique. During the eighteenth century the sultan's authority was weak and Said's decision to renew it met with some resistance from the local Arabs. But, with the assistance of the British, who saw in a restored sultanate a possible way of ending the East African slave trade, Said was successful and in 1841 transferred his capital from Muscat to Zanzibar.

Said was quick to see the commercial possibilities of his new home. By his own example, he persuaded the main landowners to develop the cultivation of cloves which quickly became Zanzibar's main industry. He issued orders that whenever a coco-nut palm was destroyed, three cloves should be planted in its place. As important, these plantations needed slave labour and this proved a powerful stimulus to the slave trade in the interior.

The sultan once told a visiting Frenchman, 'I am nothing but a merchant.' His main ambition was to make Zanzibar the entrepôt for the whole of East Africa, the capital of a flourishing economic empire. With this in mind he tended to subordinate political control along the coast to his trading designs. Krapf noted that

> the Arabs and Africans submit to his nominal pretensions so long as their own old arrangements are not too stringently interfered with. They receive the sultan's governors and pay the dues which he levies from their ports; but beyond that Seyyid Said seems to have no hope of further obedience and subjection.

It was under Said's direction that the Arab–Swahili traders began to make headway into the interior in search of slaves and ivory. Their caravans were large and well-organized affairs. Since they could often be away for as long as two years, long-term credit was needed and this was provided by Indian financiers whom Said encouraged to settle at Zanzibar. They concentrated mainly on the central route across to Lake Tanganyika although they were also active from Kilwa towards Lake Nyasa and beyond. The northerly journey from Tanga to Lake Victoria was less popular since it passed through the territory of hostile tribes like the Masai.

The scarlet Zanzibari flag carried at the head of these caravans indicated that they were under Said's protection. Probably more effective was the fact that they were well armed although this proved a declining asset as they sold guns in return for slaves and ivory. Their long absence from the coast meant that the Arabs had to establish their own settlements inland at places such as Tabora and Ujiji. These were used as bases for supplies as well as collecting-points. Their security depended on the goodwill of the local Africans and whenever possible they were the result of careful negotiations. When Burton visited Tabora he found a congenial refuge.

> The houses ... are large, substantial and capable of defence. Their gardens are extensive and well planted; they receive regular supplies of merchandise, comforts and luxuries from the coast; they are surrounded by troops of concubines and slaves whom they train to divers crafts and callings.

Because of the nature of their trade, Arab methods were seldom pleasant and more often than not left a trail of destruction behind them. They encouraged inter-tribal wars so that they could benefit from the spoils and if these failed, they were always prepared to attack directly. David Livingstone was the unwilling witness to their violence in July 1871 when they massacred a large number of Manyuema at Nyangwe on the Lualaba river. He wrote in his journal:

> After the terrible affair in the water, the party of Tagamoio, who was the chief perpetrator, continued to fire on the people there and fire their villages. As I write I hear the loud wails on the left bank over those who are slain, ignorant of their many friends now in the depths of the Lualaba. Oh, let Thy kingdom come! No one will ever know the exact loss on this bright sultry summer morning, it gave me the impression of being in Hell!

35 An ivory market in Central Africa. Ivory became the main trading commodity of the Arabs

36 An all too frequent occurrence in East and Central Africa as the Arab

Raids of this nature left widespread depopulation, unrest, and suspicion of strangers. Practically every European explorer commented on the desolation of many of the areas they visited. H. M. Stanley noted more than once how whole villages would empty in panic as his party approached since they assumed he was an Arab in search of slaves and ivory.

Said himself had his own particular difficulties in Zanzibar. The Arabs needed European assistance and goodwill and consequently a number of commercial treaties were signed with Britain, the United States, France, and Germany. As a result a number of European consulates were set up in

traders raided villages in search of ivory
and slaves

Zanzibar and Said and his successors, Majid and Barghash, found it increasingly difficult to avoid their demands.

Two British consuls, Atkins Hamerton and Sir John Kirk, were particularly influential over the question of the slave trade. In 1822, 1839, and 1845, Said was forced to accept severe limitations on the areas where slaves could be sold. The Royal Navy provided a preventive squadron but the wide stretch of coast and sea made its task difficult. The Arab merchants were prepared to use any device to evade the regulations while the other European powers, as in West Africa, tended to be lukewarm towards the

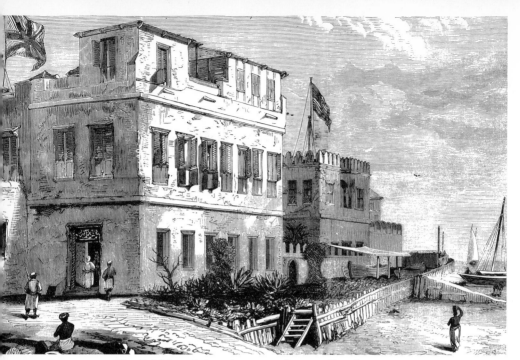

37 The British and American consulates at Zanzibar.
It was through these that the Europeans exercised
a thinly veiled paramountcy over the sultanate

British initiative. When Sir Bartle Frere visited Zanzibar in 1873 to assist
Kirk in his efforts to end the slave trade, he noted that other Europeans

> wish it left alone, not from wishing to participate in it or its profits, but because
> when the slave trade is flourishing other trade flourishes, when the slave trade
> is depressed or persecuted other trade is dull.

In June 1873 the combined efforts of Frere and Kirk were successful and
Sultan Barghash agreed to abolish the trade completely in Zanzibar, although not before he had been threatened by bombardment and blockade
by the British squadron.

This was a considerable achievement and went a long way to ending the
export of slaves but it did not stop the trade in the interior. The Scottish
missionary, A. M. Mackay, wrote with some bitterness from Lake Victoria
in 1878 that 'There are a few gunboats on the coast, and our naval nation
rests satisfied. But there is an ignorance of doings here which is not bliss . . .'

Slaves continued to be bought by the Arabs, partly for use as porters but

64

mainly for sale to other African tribes in return for ivory. Stanley became aware of the close connection between the increasing demand for ivory and the continuation of the slave trade inland. He wrote angrily:

> Every tusk, piece, and scrap of ivory in the possession of an Arab slaver has been steeped and dyed in blood. Every pound weight has cost the life of a man, woman or child; for every five pounds a hut has been burned; for every two tusks a whole village has been destroyed; every twenty tusks have been obtained at the price of a district, with all its people, villages and plantations. It is simply incredible that, because ivory is required for ornaments or billiard games, the rich heart of Africa should be laid waste . . .

Tippu Tib and Mirambo

After 1873, Sultan Barghash was in an odd and difficult position. Having destroyed most of his economic authority in Zanzibar, Kirk then proceeded to try to create a political empire for the sultan although this was something that the sultanate had never really tried to achieve. Kirk seems to have totally misunderstood the nature of the Arab régime but he thought that a

38 A late nineteenth-century photograph of slaves in East Africa. The internal trade continued for many years to provide carriers for the ivory markets

65

revival of the sultan's power might offer a cheap way of ensuring the peace of the interior as well as guaranteeing for the British a major share of the influence. It was a policy that received hardly any support in London where there was little desire to encourage any kind of East African empire whether official or not. The reaction in Zanzibar was also unenthusiastic although, during the very early stages of the scramble as German influence grew, Barghash saw some merit in Kirk's scheme.

The fact was, however, that Arab authority was too isolated and fitful to serve as any kind of useful rallying-point. Their trading methods rarely reconciled the Africans and any influence they possessed was limited in scope and short-lived. Only west of Lake Tanganyika were the Arabs able to exert any effective political control and that was a region outside the scope of Kirk's plans.

The man responsible for this lone example of successful Arab colonization was Muhammed bin Sayed, better known as Tippu Tib because of a nervous twitch of his eyes. The son of an African father and an Arab mother, he was something of a scholar and was described by Stanley as 'an Arab gentleman in very comfortable circumstances'. He began life with little more than his wits but through the ivory and slave trades he became one of the richest men in Zanzibar. In practice Tippu Tib was rarely to be found there since he had quickly decided that the best way of obtaining a

39 Sultan Barghash of Zanzibar, whose authority was not strong enough to resist the increasing influence of Europeans

66

trading monopoly was to create his own political empire far in the interior.

Tippu Tib's dominions were centred on the territory of the Manyuema between Lake Tanganyika and the Lualaba. Constantly at each other's throats, the Manyuema were easily controlled by the Arabs as they moved in during the 1860s on the simple principle of divide and rule. From his headquarters at Nyangwe, Tippu Tib soon exercised decisive control over a wide area although there were the inevitable abuses caused by his search for ivory and slaves. But Jerome Becker, a Belgian, who met him several times during the 1880s, commented:

> He enjoys an unbounded popularity, not only in his own but in the adjoining districts, where he is known as a man who would heartily disapprove of any unneighbourly act. From his immense plantations, cultivated by thousands of slaves, all blindly devoted to their master, and from his ivory trade, of which he has the monopoly, he has in his duplex character of conqueror and trader, succeeded in creating for himself in the heart of Africa a veritable empire.

In 1877, while assisting Stanley down the Congo, Tippu Tib became the first Arab to penetrate the rich ivory region of the Congolese forest. His exploitation of this new source of supply, involving much cruelty to the local tribes, inevitably turned him further westwards just at the time when the agents of Leopold II of the Belgians were pushing up the Congo in

40   Tippu Tib, the remarkable Arab–Swahili trader who virtually carved out an independent dominion in Central Africa, just before the scramble

41 Mirambo, the Nyamwezi leader, who tried
to challenge the Arab control of the East
African trade routes

their attempts to establish the Congo Free State. During Stanley's last
expedition (1885–89), Tippu Tib was appointed governor of the upper
Congo on behalf of the new state on the expedient grounds that he alone
had any authority there.

It was from Tippu Tib's point of view a more sensible appointment than
the one offered to him in 1883 by Barghash. The sultan had hoped he would
take control over a virtually non-existent area of Arab influence stretching
to the east of Lake Tanganyika. Had Tippu Tib accepted, he would inevitably have clashed with the great Nyamwezi leader, Mirambo, who
during the 1870s and early 1880s practically controlled the whole of what
is now central Tanzania. Tippu Tib once claimed improbably that they
were both related and, whether true or not, they certainly had a great deal
in common. Both wanted political dominions and control of the local trade
routes. In Mirambo's case this was bound to lead to a head-on collision
with the Arabs, all of whom he detested except for Tippu Tib who had
earned his respect and whose caravans he allowed to pass unmolested.

Mirambo's régime was the inevitable culmination of the clash between the Arabs and the older East African traders, the Nyamwezi. But even if the growing European involvement had not lessened the influence of both, it is doubtful if the Nyamwezi could have held their initiative for long. They could make it difficult and at times impossible for the Arabs to conduct their business but in the end the sultan had one considerable advantage in his ability to close most of the ports to Nyamwezi trade.

Mirambo's authority, however, was sufficiently impressive for Kirk to consider him as a possible counterweight should his Arab plans fail. It was only the death of two Englishmen during a Nyamwezi raid in 1880 that turned him against Mirambo. The Nyamwezi leader was certainly an impressive man. E. J. Southon, an English missionary who worked in his territory, has left an account of his methods:

> He generally timed his marches so as to arrive in the night, and about an hour before daybreak a furious assault was mounted. The chief of the village was then put to death . . . and his immediate successor appointed to rule in his stead. The new chief was required to swear allegiance to Mirambo and a number of youths selected to recruit his army.

Once an area was subjugated, Mirambo then ruled

> with a moderation and wisdom seldom seen in a native prince . . . The new chiefs were praised, flattered and extolled . . . The commons were treated in a similar manner; new rights and privileges were given which raised them far above their former degraded serfdom . . .

There was, however, a fatal flaw in Mirambo's system. Stanley described him as 'the African Bonaparte' and it was only through war that he could keep his ever-expanding army contented. He had some similarities to a medieval *condottiere*, ever on the move searching for new enemies. As in all military régimes, much depended on the personality of the leader and the continuance of victories. During the early 1880s an illness caused by an abscess of the throat began to sap his energy and lessened his control. Inevitably, rival chiefs began to jockey for power. At the same time Mirambo was involved in some unpleasant quarrels with the Ngoni whom he had previously used as allies. These were groups of warriors who had broken away from the control of Shaka's Zulus far to the south and had begun to trek northwards. Collecting the remnants of those through whose territory they had passed, they caused considerable havoc as they raided and pillaged their way towards Lake Tanganyika. Although far from reliable friends, the Ngoni had taught Mirambo a number of lessons. Not only had they adapted the highly successful military tactics of the Zulus, they had also in their long journey north developed a system of uniting different tribes into coherent and powerful units. In building his own personal empire, Mirambo benefited from these influences. Nevertheless, his achievements were largely his own. He was a remarkable figure who had managed to stamp his personality over a large area of East Africa. His epitaph was written by the one-time missionary and later gun-runner, Charles Stokes: 'Mirambo was a most wonderful man. I know not his equal throughout the country. A wise ruler, a grand general for native warfare, every inch a soldier.'

Tippu Tib and Mirambo had come near to controlling the almost chaotic situation that the slavers and ivory-hunters had caused throughout much of East Africa. But they were themselves exploiters and an integral part of the system of trade that had grown up. Its abuses were most unlikely to be ended by men so closely involved. It seemed as if only Europeans could achieve this task and by the 1880s their influence was increasingly apparent in many parts of East Africa. A sad and disillusioned Barghash wrote apologetically to Tippu Tib in 1886

> I must beg your forgiveness. I no longer have any hope of keeping the interior. The Europeans here in Zanzibar are after my possessions. Will it be the hinterland they want? Happy are those who died before now, and know nothing of this.

The Lake States

During the nineteenth century the comparatively sophisticated lake states to the west and north of Lake Victoria were increasingly drawn into contact with the outside world. The most significant influence proved to be that of Europeans but earlier the Arab–Swahili traders had begun to penetrate the area while to the north Egyptian pressure down the Nile made itself felt.

The most important of the states were Ruanda, Bunyoro, and Buganda. Warfare between them and their far from negligible neighbours, Karagwe, Ankole, and Urundi, was common although the results frequently seemed indecisive. During the second half of the century, Kigeri, ruler of Ruanda, reorganized his army so that not all the regiments were engaged in every campaign. The result was that he had a continuous stream of fresh warriors for almost permanent fighting. In the course of his wars, he added no new territory to his kingdom but managed to increase his prestige and influence in the best way possible, by gaining cattle.

The whole area round Lake Victoria was free from the tsetse-fly and so eminently suitable for cattle farming. Large-scale rustling of the kind that Kigeri was almost continuously engaged in was one important motive for fighting. As significant, however, was the constant interference in the succession disputes of neighbouring states. In nearly all the lake states except Buganda, the death of a ruler involved often bitter civil wars between the different heirs and claimants for the throne. Larger neighbours often cultivated their own clients in the hope of gaining at best an ally and at worst a satellite. This was the favourite method employed by Buganda in expanding her own frontiers. The kingdom of Toro was especially vunerable since it became the target not only of the Ganda but also of Bunyoro.

By the middle of the nineteenth century, Bunyoro was well on the way to recovering from a long period of commercial and political weakness. To European visitors, it appeared a less well-ordered state than Buganda, its *omukama* possessing none of the *kabaka's* dignity. When J. H. Speke and J. A. Grant visited Bunyoro in 1862 they were far from impressed. Speke wrote:

> Nothing could be more filthy than the state of the palace, and all the lanes leading up to it: it was well, perhaps, that we were never expected to go there, for without stilts and respirators it would have been impracticable, such is the dirty nature of the people.

In fact they misunderstood the nature of the Bunyoro system of government. It was a large state with a number of smaller client chiefs on its borders. The *omukama*, therefore, had no fixed capital and moved round his empire on permanent safari. This itinerant method of government may not always have guaranteed the *omukama's* comfort but it did enable him to keep his eye on all his subjects.

Under two rulers, Kamurasi and Kabarega, Bunyoro became a powerful state. They were able to control the trade from the area of Lakes Albert and Kyoga and, exploiting its iron-ore potential, obtained guns both from Zanzibar and Khartoum. They were able as a result effectively to check Buganda's expansion while deterring the Egyptian advance down the Nile under a succession of European commanders, Sir Samuel Baker, General Charles Gordon, and the German, Emin Pasha. During the 1890s, Bunyoro

42   The main residence of the *kabakas* of Buganda
gives an impression of the power and authority
of the Lake States

43   Mutesa, *kabaka*
of Buganda

eventually collapsed before the advancing British but not before Kabarega
had proved himself a brave and intelligent guerilla general.

Buganda had one distinct advantage over its neighbours in that its
climate and soil normally meant that there was no serious crisis as far as
food production was concerned. This material wealth was the basis of the
state's strength and stability. Ultimately everything was dependent on the
kabaka and during the greater part of the nineteenth century there were
only three, Suna (1831–56), Mutesa (1856–84), and Mwanga (1884–99).
Unlike the other lake states, the *kabakas* rarely had to indulge in civil war
against possible rivals if only because they were quick to eliminate them.
European visitors were fascinated as well as repelled by these rulers. The
missionary, Robert Ashe, wrote of Mutesa that he was

> kindly but formal, fearful of his dignity, crafty, suspicious, and capable of acts
> so vile and foul that they may only be hinted at, surrounded by an abject court,
> an object of grovelling adoration to slavish thousands.

The Ganda themselves were less critical of this kind of régime than the
Europeans but there were occasions when they felt able to express their

44 Mutesa, surrounded by his courtiers, giving
an audience to Speke and Grant, the first
Europeans to visit Buganda

own fears and doubts. At the funeral of the tyrannical Suna, it is claimed,
his pall-bearers threw his body to the ground in contemptuous disgust.

Mutesa inherited from his father a powerful kingdom which he further
strengthened by a series of important administrative reforms. The influence of the old priesthood was severely limited while the already powerful
central bureaucracy was made still stronger. Deputies were sent out into
the various districts where they quickly usurped the authority of the local
chiefs. The system was further reinforced by the recruiting agents of the
newly organized army, increasingly supplied by the Arabs with guns. To a
greater degree than any other part of Africa outside the Oil River states and
Shaka's Zulu kingdom, Mutesa's organization opened up a career to all
talents. Rank and prestige were subordinated to ability and it was possible
for a commoner to rise to the highest office. This no doubt furthered the
stability of Buganda although it was often precarious for those concerned.
Ashe wrote of one powerful chief whose behaviour was like that of the
ruler himself:

But his peers do not forget that though he is an earl today, he is a mere mush-
room nobleman, a parvenu, a peasant. Only a few years ago he was but a miser-
able drummer.

73

Although the warfare of many of the lake states was in part geared to the need to obtain food, especially cattle, Buganda, paradoxically, tended to wage war for precisely the opposite reason. The comparative abundance of good farming land meant that much of the agriculture could be left to women while the men went off to fight. This somewhat pointless exercise began, however, to have its more sinister motives as the nineteenth century progressed. Unlike Bunyoro, with her iron trade, Buganda's wealth included little that was suitable for export. Once the Arab traders began to penetrate the area during the 1840s, slaves and ivory were needed if the Ganda were to have the guns, cottons, and silks that they wanted from Zanzibar. What began as a frivolous branch of the Arab luxury trade soon turned Buganda into one of the most important slaving states of East Africa. The armies of Buganda devastated large tracts of the immediate neighbourhood while its fleet of high-prowed canoes dominated Lake Victoria and the people who lived round its shore.

Arab influence grew in importance in Buganda. Trade was their main preoccupation but they also introduced Islam and an increasing awareness of the outside world. They were the precursors of alien influences that were to test the structure of Ganda society during the remaining years of the century.

Buganda and the Missions

The first Europeans to visit Buganda were Speke and Grant in 1862. For a dozen years there were no more although Mutesa was anxiously aware of the possible danger from Equatoria, the southernmost province of the Egyptian Sudan with its succession of European governors. It was partly in the hope of securing a counterweight to this possible threat that he welcomed Stanley in 1875. Stanley was charmed by Buganda in general and the *kabaka* in particular.

> I found Mutesa, not a tyrannous savage, a wholesale murderer, but a pious Mussulman and an intelligent human king reigning absolutely over a vast section of Africa, loved more than hated, respected more than feared, of all his subjects.

In spite of the obvious influence of the Arabs and Islam, Stanley saw Buganda as a fruitful field for missionary activity. Mutesa agreed, hoping

74

that a Christian mission might be of practical use to him. The first party of the Church Missionary Society reached Buganda in 1876, its leader, A. M. Mackay, taking a more sombre view of the *kabaka* than Stanley:

> A king that is used to nothing but flattery from his courtiers, whose lives he can take at any moment if they do anything other than flatter him, is no ordinary individual to speak plainly to. One needs a smooth tongue when speaking to him.

The situation was complicated by the arrival a few weeks later of some of Cardinal Lavigerie's Catholic White Fathers. This introduced a note of petty sectarian bitterness that confused Mutesa and enabled the Arabs, fearful for their trading interests in Buganda, to play one mission off against the other. In spite of these difficulties, however, both Protestants and Catholics made a substantial number of converts whose new-found faith was to be sorely tried after Mutesa's death in 1884.

'This tyrant is rash and vain,' wrote Mackay of the new *kabaka*, Mwanga, 'and fancies that there is no power in the world that can call his vilest and most cruel acts in question.' The *kabaka* particularly resented the influence of the Christian converts at court, afraid that through them the missions were undermining his authority. The increasing political role on the coast of the British and the Germans only served to increase Mwanga's anxieties.

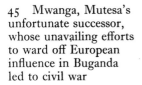

45 Mwanga, Mutesa's unfortunate successor, whose unavailing efforts to ward off European influence in Buganda led to civil war

75

In 1885 he interpreted the appointment of John Hannington to a new bishopric in Buganda as the spearhead of a new and more powerful European advance and promptly had him murdered before he could arrive. The following year he had killed some fifty to a hundred Christian courtiers, some of them among his most intelligent advisers. It was a tribute to the remaining Ganda Christians that under these difficult circumstances they remained faithful to the missions.

Mwanga's behaviour soon alienated most of the leading chiefs and courtiers who began to associate with the Catholics and Protestants as well as with the Arabs to form political parties and factions. The religious loyalties of these different groups tended to become obscured as they vied with each other to seize the authority that the *kabaka* was so patently abusing. Mwanga was little more than a pawn and a puppet during a complicated series of civil wars that were only ended by the active intervention of the Imperial British East Africa Company. By 1894 Buganda and much of the surrounding neighbourhood had become the British Protectorate of Uganda.

What was most significant about this sad period of Buganda's history was less the extraordinary nature of the warring factions than the continuing strength of its institutions. Because of the reforms of Suna and Mutesa, the country had developed a degree of flexibility that enabled its people to absorb alien cultures and rule without ever losing their basic African

46   From a missionary viewpoint, this photograph suggests a happy ending. Taken just before 1914, it shows the Christian rulers of Bunyoro, Buganda, Ankole, and Toro united under the British flag

47 An ebony carving of the
head of a Masai girl

identity. The missions had penetrated deep into Buganda and had been
partly responsible for creating a near-revolutionary situation. But the
basic characteristics of Ganda society, far from being destroyed, had been
tested and strengthened, suggesting perhaps that Stanley's optimistic view
of Buganda and its people was near to the truth.

The Tribes of Kenya

In 1901 a railway linking Mombasa with Lake Victoria was completed
through British East Africa, the territory subsequently known as Kenya.
At first this area seemed important only as a link between Uganda and the
sea. Compared with the lake states and even the region to the south, this
was a hostile land. The Arabs always regarded it as a second-best route to
the Lakes, a view confirmed by the British railway-builders.

The dominating tribe was the Masai who occupied most of the Rift
Valley. Their main delights were fighting and cattle and they were constantly
at war with their neighbours and each other. Fierce nomads, they resented
external intrusion and consequently had changed little over the centuries.
Far-eastern traders in the ninth century left a description that was still
accurate in the nineteenth.

77

They often stick a needle into the veins of cattle and draw blood which they drink raw, mixed with milk. They wear no clothes except that they cover below their loins with sheepskins. Their women are clean and chaste.

By the second half of the nineteenth century, the Masai were less formidable as they became decimated by constant in-fighting and by disease that affected their cattle as well as themselves. Joseph Thompson, the explorer, owed his passage through Masailand in 1883 to his skill at coping with a cattle epidemic. But he noted the sad state of the area.

The whole country presented a fearful spectacle of skeletons and dried skins, which told eloquently a tale of disease and death. The scourge had found its way from the plateau, and had hardly left a head of cattle in the entire country.

The relative decline of the Masai allowed both the Kikuyu and the Kamba to expand. The former lived in the highlands running south from Mount Kenya. For years they had been hemmed in by the Masai but during the second half of the nineteenth century they began to break out of their narrowly defined areas. Mainly arable farmers, they cut down the thick forests and pushed on as far as the edge of the Kenya plain. It was during this time that they purchased land from the near-by Dorobo, an arrangement which the British officials and settlers at first misunderstood and which was to cause the Kikuyu serious irritation in later years. They traded mainly among themselves and discouraged merchants from outside. Passing close to their territory, Thompson had no desire to inquire too closely into their affairs. He commented that they 'had the reputation of being the most troublesome and intractable people in this region'.

The Kamba occupied the area between the Kikuyu and the sea. They were active traders, competing with the Arabs for control of the local routes. Like the Masai and the Kikuyu, there was no settled political pattern and no obvious paramount chief. Among all these tribes, leadership in war sometimes brought a man into temporary prominence, but more often it was the priests and those who claimed to have magic skills who exercised the most influence. Krapf noted this among the Kamba.

Wealth, a ready flow of language, an imposing personal appearance, and, above all, the reputation for being a magician and rain-maker, are the surest means by which a Mkamba can attain power and importance and secure the obedience of his countrymen.

78

48 The railway between the coast and Lake Victoria was completed in 1901, encouraging white settlement in Kenya. Many of the Indians brought over to help build the line remained as traders

At the time of the partition it seemed probable that all these peoples might become involved in serious inter-tribal wars. The British occupation of the area lessened the immediate tensions but at the same time brought in new ones. The first white settlers arrived in Kenya in 1902 in the footsteps of the Indian coolies who had helped to build the Uganda railway. They gave to the area new possibilities of commercial and agricultural wealth that were eventually to make Kenya the richest part of East Africa. At the same time they introduced landholding and racial problems that were not at first apparent but which were in the end to lead to bitterness and misery on both sides.

79

4 West Central Africa

THE HISTORY OF the enormous area bounded by the Congo river and its tributaries is less well known than that of any other part of tropical Africa. In the north lies the thick equatorial forest, the home of the pygmies among other tribes. Along the rivers the population has always been fairly dense although the forest meant that many, like the Manyuema in the Lualaba area, lived in semi-isolated village communities. In the south where the forest thins out into savanna as far as the upper reaches of the Zambesi, there developed a number of powerful and well-organized states.

The Katanga part of the region was already famous throughout Central Africa for its mineral deposits, particularly copper. But the formative influence both economically and politically was the trade in slaves and ivory. The main demand from outside came originally from Europeans, especially the Portuguese, who had early in the sixteenth century established bases on both the west and east coasts. By the nineteenth century, however, both the Nyamwezi and the Arabs from East Africa had been attracted to the area in their search for slaves and ivory.

The Kongo and Angola

By 1800 the ancient Kongo kingdom to the south of the Congo estuary was a mere fragment of what had at one time been a great African state. A Catholic priest described its ruler during the sixteenth century as 'a king of kings who is the absolute lord of all his realm'. It was through the influence of Portuguese missions that the Kongo made a genuine attempt to accept the Christian faith and some of the outward trappings of European life. Unfortunately, the growing interest of the Portuguese in slaves destroyed this development and began steadily to undermine the authority of the Kongo's rulers. One king, Affonso, wrote bitterly to Portugal in 1526 to explain that

49   An eighteenth-century print of the king
of the Kongo. By the nineteenth century,
the authority of the ruler of the Kongo
was more apparent than real

there are many traders in all corners of the kingdom. They bring ruin to the country. Every day people are enslaved and kidnapped, even nobles, even members of the king's own family.

It was to the advantage of the Portuguese slavers to encourage inter-tribal fighting and consequently by the eighteenth century the Kongo was reduced to warring factions. This completed the erosion of royal authority that had begun with the original attempt to accept the alien customs of the Europeans. Nevertheless, the old traditions of the Kongo kings still retained a tenuous influence since the great majority of the petty chiefs still proudly claimed descent from Affonso as late as 1800.

Although the Congo river remained an important source of slaves until well into the nineteenth century, the largest number was supplied by the Portuguese colony of Angola further down the coast. Discarding the half-hearted kind of partnership they had had with the Kongo kingdom, the

81

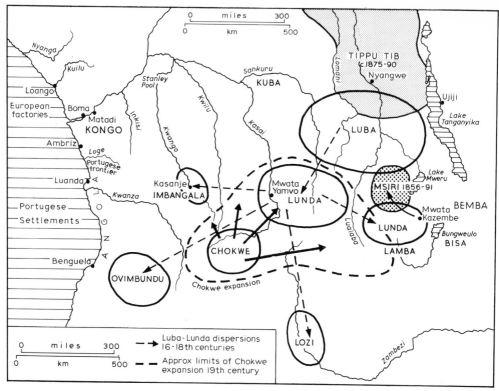

MAP NO. 5
West Central Africa, 1800–80, tribal areas and migrations

Portuguese tried to occupy Angola as a colony from the very beginning. This involved them in a series of bitter wars throughout the seventeenth century with the local inhabitants, the Mbundu and their allies, the Jagas and the Ovimbundu. African resistance was successful enough to confine the Portuguese to a narrow coastal strip with two important ports, Luanda and Benguela. Not until the last quarter of the nineteenth century when the scramble was at its height were the Portuguese able to extend their control into the interior. But, although territorially the colony of Angola was minute, its prosperity had to be measured in the large number of slaves exported annually to Brazil. The effects of this trade were to be felt deep into the interior where few Europeans were to be seen before the middle of the nineteenth century.

The Inland States

As in West Africa, the slave trade of the west central region was conducted by middlemen who acted as a link between the European traders on the coast and the great slaving states of the interior. Two groups of people, the Mbundu and the Lunda, were to play important roles in this development.

Both had organized skeleton kingships before the arrival of the Portuguese on the coast. The Mbundu owed a great deal to the example of the Kongo kingdom to the north while, several hundred miles inland, the Lunda were influenced by their Luba neighbours in upper Katanga. The heartland of the Mbundu became part of Portuguese Angola but refugees under the inspired leadership of Queen Nzinga established a new state of Matamba to the north-east. Before her death Nzinga became a Christian but this seems to have implied equality with rather than subservience to the Portuguese. Matamba soon became an important clearing-house for slaves with the Lunda states of the interior, rivalled only by neighbouring Kasanje a state set up during the seventeenth century by some Lunda immigrants from the east who conquered and absorbed the Imbangala.

Kasanje was the western tip of Lunda expansion that had its origins as far back as the sixteenth century. In the depths of the savanna of Central Africa, groups of tribesmen had begun to move away from the original Luba empire. For more than a century after 1600, these migrants had pushed west, south, and east in an area with few natural boundaries. While the Imbangala were being conquered in the west, the Bemba had moved east and others had settled over large areas of south-east Katanga and the Rhodesian plateau. Their frontiers were vague and frequently overlapped but by the eighteenth century the two most important Lunda nations were Mwata Yamvo and to its south-east Mwata Kazembe. These were large, well-organized, and sophisticated states whose rulers were considered divine.

These great savanna states and the others grouped round them were centres for a vigorous local trade but their main concern was in the business of collecting and selling slaves through Mbundu and Kasanje in return for guns and other European goods. The Portuguese themselves normally held aloof from direct trading entrusting it to the *pombeiros*, negro or mulatto agents who negotiated with the Mbundu and the Imbangala from Kasanje.

83

These men were universally unpopular. James Johnston, an English explorer, passed the grave of a *pombeiro* in a remote part of Angola during the early 1890s:

> The natives had with grim satire erected a monument to his memory, by stringing some twenty of these shackles on a pole and sticking it up at the head of a mound . . . Numerous bleaching skulls a little way from the track tell how the slaves whom death has set free are disposed of. But the headman of an ordinary caravan is generally buried in a very respectful manner, his hat, his umbrella, cooking-pot, and powder barrel being invariably placed on the grave.

The Collapse of the Kingdoms

For the first half of the nineteenth century, West Central Africa continued to be dominated by the kingdoms of Mwata Yamvo and Mwata Kazembe. Kazembe in particular, astride the Luapula river, was practically in the centre of the continent and so able to trade with both the west and east coasts. Its trade with the Portuguese settlements round the mouth of the Zambesi was mainly in ivory though some slaving seems to have taken place. As in the west, there was little direct contact between the Africans of the interior and the Portuguese on the coast. The Bisa people to the south-east of Kazembe were used as carriers negotiating with *pombeiros* at the Portuguese station at Tete on the Zambesi.

The Portuguese were anxious to diminish the control of the African middlemen and to obtain more direct influence over the trans-continental routes. During the early years of the century they sent more than one exploratory expedition inland. In 1806 two *pombeiros* managed to cross from Luanda to Tete and back. One of them left an account of Mwata Kazembe where he and his companion were imprisoned for the best part of four years.

> When there are no travellers trading at his capital, he [the king] will order slaves and ivory to be collected, and will go with his ambassadors to chastise such chiefs as stop the way to traders coming from Tete to his country. The territory of Kazembe is supplied with provisions all the year round – manioc flour, millet, maize, beans, bananas, sugar-canes, potatoes, yams, gourds, ground-nuts, and much fish from the rivers . . . King Kazembe has tea-pots, cups, silver spoons and forks . . . He has a Christian courtesy: he doffs his cap and gives good day.

By the middle of the nineteenth century this settled pattern of trade from both east and west had been interrupted and the kingdoms of Mwata Kazambe and Mwata Yamvo had collapsed. In part this was due, especially in the west, to changing trading demands as European pressure forced an end to the slave trade. Equally important, however, was the arrival of new traders and the intrusion into west Central Africa of the Nyamwezi and the Arabs.

The trade to the east coast began to be forced north away from the line of the Zambezi towards the Central Lakes and Zanzibar. Some responsibility for this must be attached to the incursions of the Ngoni in the region round Lake Nyasa. But far more significant was the advance of the Nyamwezi and Arab traders beyond the Central Lakes in search of new ivory and slave areas. Although the Arabs pushed their caravans down as far south as Katanga, they in the main exploited the country immediately

50   The ruler of Mwata Kazembe

to the west of Lake Tanganyika. The dominions of Tippu Tib were the main result of this penetration.

Of greater significance for the future of Kazembe were the Nyamwezi traders (known locally as Bayeke) who began to push into the area in considerable force during the 1840s and 1850s. They came originally for copper and other minerals and a number of them settled in Kazembe to organize the trade. One of these was Kalasa who made frequent journeys into Katanga and left his son Msiri there as his permanent agent. It marked the end of Mwata Kazembe.

Msiri was not content to act as a simple trader. Using the growing bands of Nyamwezi in the area, he established his headquarters at Bunkeya in the northern part of Kazembe. Well-organized and brutal, he soon controlled most of the country between the Lualaba and the Luapula rivers. Faced by this determined invasion over a period of years, the central authority of Mwata Kazembe collapsed and the chiefs of the area were forced to pay tribute to Msiri. His empire became a flourishing centre dealing in ivory, copper, and salt. The British explorer, V. L. Cameron, had no doubt 'that many of Msiri's men have visited both coasts, and that a message might be sent by these people from Benguela to Zanzibar'.

Cameron's confidence was a tribute to Msiri's real authority over a large portion of west Central Africa. It was, however, a cruel and tyrannical rule. The Scottish missionary, F. S. Arnott, who reached Bunkeya in 1886, wrote:

> Hearing him talk of his wars, and seeing all round his yard human skulls . . . the sensation creeps over one of being in a monster's den . . . He has the name of being very kind among his people, but at the same time very strict. He does not stop at taking their heads off.

Msiri's own brand of justice certainly had its own distinctive logic. Of thieves, he said, 'I stab them in the heart because the hand never stole anything. It is the heart who is the thief.' Blinding an adulterer was not enough. 'The real eyes are in the heart and death is the only true blindness.'

During the scramble, Msiri's empire became the target for both Cecil Rhodes's British South Africa Company and the agents of Leopold II's Congo Free State. Both were attracted by the rich mineral deposits there, particularly the copper. Rhodes gave Joseph Thomson the urgent message 'to get Msiri's . . . I mean Katanga . . . You must go and get Katanga.'

86

51 Msiri, brooding and brutal, effectively destroyed Mwata Kazembe, establishing his own trading empire in Central Africa until it too was destroyed by agents of Leopold II

In the event it was Leopold's men who seized the prize in 1891 when they usurped Msiri's authority after his death in a scuffle with a Belgian officer.

Meanwhile there had been equally important changes on the west coast. The long connection between Angola and Brazil continued well into the nineteenth century. In 1838 slavery was officially declared illegal in all Portuguese colonies although in both Angola and Mozambique officials connived at its continuance. The export of slaves to Brazil, however, became more difficult as international pressure made itself felt. This seriously affected the prosperity of Luanda and the Imbangala traders inland who organized much of the trade. The main consequence was to increase the importance of the port of Benguela as a centre for the ivory trade. The intermediaries here were the Ovimbundu, like the Imbangala, originally organized by Lunda invaders, but by the nineteenth century a haven of refuge for the rag, tag, and bobtail of Angolan society. Escaped slaves

52 A Lozi village in the Barotse plain. Their well-developed
institutions enabled them to survive as a coherent group
during an unsettled period in Central African history

and prisoners joined deserters from the Portuguese army and made the
Ovimbundu the most unscrupulous but determined of African traders
in the area.

In their search for ivory, the Ovimbundu relied to a large extent on their
immediate neighbours to the east, the Chokwe. Before the middle of the
nineteenth century, the Chokwe were virtually unknown. David Livingstone passed through their territory in 1854 at a time when they were

already beginning to expand. He was told that they 'were familiar with the visits of slave traders, and it was the opinion of our guides that so many of my companions would be demanded of me that I should reach the coast without a single attendant'.

The Chokwe became specialist ivory-hunters. The Ovimbundu kept them well supplied with guns in return for the ivory and encouraged them to exploit systematically one region after another. It was a rapid expansion that by the 1880s had reached Mwata Yamvo. Like Mwata Kazembe to the east, the old kingdom was unable to withstand these new pressures and collapsed under the strain.

Only in isolated areas were the remnants of the Lunda people able to preserve something of their former prosperity. A German explorer, Leo Frobenius, was surprised in 1901 to find villages along the Kasai

> whose principal streets were lined on both sides . . . with four rows of palm trees . . . Everywhere there were velvets and silken stuffs. Every cup, every pipe, every spoon was a piece of artistry, fully worthy of comparison with the creations of Europe.

But in the same year, Colonel C. Harding, travelling across the Congo-Zambezi watershed, noted a far sadder and probably more common situation. He wrote that owing to slaving 'the Lunda are in a constant state of armed resistance. Most of the villages are stockaded, and on our arrival the natives rushed away into the bush like rabbits . . .'

Central Africa north of the Zambezi

The confused situation existing in the Congo was repeated in the area to the south-east covered by the modern states of Malawi, Zambia, and northern Botswana. Many of its people had long and close contacts with the Luba-Lunda states of the Congo through the migration of the Bemba, Bisa, Lozi, and others. These large tribes formed a great arc stretching along the south of the Lunda states from the flood plain of the Zambesi above the Victoria Falls to the southern tip of Lake Tanganyika. Some, like the Bisa, were an integral part of the Lunda trading complex. Others were more independent.

The Lozi, for example, had developed a highly efficient political system that allowed them to dominate most of the Barotse plain. Under the greatest of their paramount chiefs, Mulambwa (1812–30), laws were passed regulating normal contingencies such as the collection of taxes but in addition provisions were made for the care of relatives of those killed in battle. During his reign slavers approached from the west but Mulambwa refused to have any dealings with them. The area under his rule was probably the best organized in Central and southern Africa. It was, therefore, a tragedy that on his death there should have been a disputed succession. Divided between themselves, the Lozi were unable to withstand the invading Kololo, part of the restless movement of people set in motion by Zulu expansion in the south. But Kololo control was only to be temporary. In 1865 the Lozi rose successfully against their new rulers and re-established much of the old order. In the more settled period of the last years of the century and under the particular guidance of Lewanika, paramount chief from 1884 to 1916, the Lozi were allowed once again to become a stable and successful nation.

Far to the north-east, another body of Lunda migrants, the Bemba, finally settled on the plateau to the south of Lake Tanganyika. It was a sparce and infertile area, forcing the Bemba to wage aggressive and expansionist wars to win their livelihood. Failing to wrest control of the Kazembe trade route from the Bisa, they found an alternative outlet northwards through contact with Arab traders from Zanzibar. This was a useful arrangement for them since they were able to obtain guns in return for their prisoners, previously a liability and normally killed. In turn this not only allowed the Bemba to organize fresh conquests but also enabled them more effectively than others to resist and defeat the Ngoni regiments from the south.

It was one of the tragedies of this region that the slave trade played such a prominent part in its history at this particular time. It was encouraged not only by the Arabs but by the Portuguese in Mozambique who were prepared to ignore all anti-slave-trade legislation as long as they could find a market for slaves. Along the eastern shores of Lake Nyasa, the Yao chiefs were able to dominate their less strong neighbours and to turn the area into an enormous source of slaves. Livingstone, passing by the lake during 1861, was particularly offended by the sheer arrogance of the slavers whom he met. He encountered a caravan led by Yaos who

> armed with muskets and bedecked with various articles of finery, marched jauntily in the front, middle and rear of the line, some of them blowing exultant notes on long tin horns . . . They seemed to feel that they were doing a very noble thing.

In the middle of the century, the Lake Nyasa region was also disrupted by the Ngoni, some of whom pushed on still further towards Lake Tanganyika, others settling in some of the best farming areas. Once the initial shock had been absorbed, it could be argued that the Ngoni provided something of a stabilizing influence. They were well-organized groups and, although preserving many of their distinctive characteristics, they intermarried easily with the tribes they had conquered. Equally important, since most of their needs were met by the area they had occupied, they rarely engaged in the slave trade although warfare remained an abiding habit.

Missionary Influence

By 1914 the whole of this vast area of Central Africa from the Congo and Angola across the continent to the mouth of the Zambezi was under European control. Relations with the Africans were often the cause of

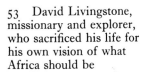

53 David Livingstone, missionary and explorer, who sacrificed his life for his own vision of what Africa should be

54 Livingstone is welcomed at a village near the Lualaba river.
Unlike many other European explorers, he had time to dwell
among the peoples he met

serious misgivings among humanitarians. In Angola and the Congo they
had every reason for alarm since the white officials there were guilty of
considerable abuse. Fortunately, there were other areas where European
influence had a more benevolent effect, particularly in what became
Nyasaland and Barotseland where the missionary presence was already
important before the arrival of traders and administrators.

The increasing missionary activity in East and Central Africa during the
latter half of the nineteenth century was the result of a number of factors.
The long tradition in Britain of opposition to the slave trade remained
active and there was a genuine desire both there and in other countries of
Europe to end the trade in the central and eastern parts of Africa.
Humanitarian alarm was further increased by the kind of reports that they
received from Africa. In general terms the explorers and others tended to
put a heavy emphasis on the brutality and barbarity of much that they
had seen. They were rarely long enough in one area to notice that beneath
the confusion there was a basic order in African society that events temporarily had tended to obscure. Livingstone, while deploring the cruelty that

92

clearly existed, was one of the few able to understand something of the real nature of African life, to recognize its natural dignity, and to hope for a more settled future. But for Livingstone the first necessity was some form of European assistance. He warned, however, that although this task was urgent, it had to be tempered with good sense and a proper realization of the real needs of the Africans. He wrote:

> If we call the actual amount of conversions the direct result of Missions, and the wide diffusion of better principles the indirect, I have no hesitation in asserting that the latter are of infinitely more importance than the former.

It was when they followed this particular proposition that the missions were able to play a significant role in the development of Central African society.

The truth of this was underlined by an early missionary failure that paradoxically Livingstone himself had actively encouraged. The major consequence of his report on the situation round Lake Nyasa was the decision to set up the Universities Mission to Central Africa. In 1861 Livingstone established its first station under Bishop Mackenzie in the Shire valley near the lake. Understandably but mistakenly the mission saw a group of slaves that they had freed as a heaven-sent nucleus of a Christian community. The local Yao slave raiders saw the position in rather more simple and brutal terms as a direct threat to their way of life. Such a situation inevitably led to fighting and, after Mackenzie's death from fever, the mission was withdrawn in 1863 to Zanzibar. There were similar failures for basically the same reasons among the Ndebele of Matabeleland and the Kololo in Barotseland.

The collapse of these early missionary ventures was not due simply to their too eager desire to gain quick conversions or to the natural antagonism of the local African rulers. They were frequently badly equipped and had made insufficient arrangements for new supplies or were unable to withstand the climate and disease. By the late 1870s, however, the situation was changing. Not least important was a significant change in the attitude of the Africans themselves. Europeans were no longer strangers and were less likely to be mistaken for Arab slavers or Portuguese *pombeiros*. The missionaries too, partly as a result of Livingstone's attitude, were now more sympathetic and understanding. There was as a result a startling contrast between the methods of the missions of the early 1860s and those of the late 1870s and 1880s.

93

François Coillard, for example, established a French Protestant mission among the Lozi of Barotseland not long after they had overthrown the Kololo. There he became a close friend and adviser of Lewanika, the paramount chief. They came to rely on each other and both showed a sensible willingness to compromise. Lewanika, for reasons of state, felt it impossible to abandon his own pagan beliefs but allowed his son to be baptized. Gradually the excesses of traditional Lozi religious practice were removed without altering the basic pattern of society and without any loss of confidence in Coillard. In the aftermath of the scramble, concession hunters, including Rhodes' agents, began to badger Lewanika. Coillard made it absolutely clear that his first duty was to serve the best interests of the Lozi and it was on his advice that they accepted British protection.

Similarly, there was a marked difference between the initial failure of Mackenzie's mission to Lake Nyasa and the success of the Scottish missions established there in the late 1870s. Dr Robert Laws had founded a station at Livingstonia on the north-west side of the lake where he was surrounded by the Tonga, currently terrorized by the neighbouring Ngoni settlers. The local Ngoni chief, apprehensive at the presence of Europeans and at the same time annoyed that they had deprived him of some prestige by settling outside his dominions, asked Laws, 'Why do you not come up and live with us? Can you milk fish? We will give you cattle. We are the rulers.' A situation of this nature demanded all Laws's tact and diplomacy to avoid an open and probably disastrous breach but significantly by the late 1880s there were already signs of a changed attitude among the local Africans. Most important was the steady return of the Tonga and others who had earlier fled from the Ngoni attacks. Sir Harry Johnston, the British consul in the area, wrote of Laws:

> This man, with his fifteen years of whole-hearted devotion to Nyasaland, and his energy of doing good which has made him learn to make bricks himself in order that he may teach others, which has led him to become a practical carpenter, joiner, printer, photographer, farrier, boat-builder, engineer and druggist . . . which had made him study medicine and surgery to heal the bodies, and sufficient theology to instruct the minds of these Africans, about whom he never speaks silly sentiments and gush, but whose faults, failings and capabilities he appraises with calm common sense – Dr Laws with these qualities of truly Christian self-devotion should justly be regarded as the greatest man who has yet appeared in Nyasaland.

To the south of the lake in the Shire highlands was another successful

Scottish mission at Blantyre. Like Mackenzie's earlier venture in the same region, this one too had almost failed through its uncompromising attitude towards the Yaos. A new leader, the Reverend David Scott, saved the situation by his practical good sense. When, in 1891, a German missionary visited Blantyre what impressed him most were the practical achievements that had been made, while Johnston was moved to call the station an 'English Arcadia'. Both the Scottish missions were supported by the African Lakes Corporation founded with the double purpose of bringing in supplies and taking out ivory at a price which would undercut that of the Arabs and the Portuguese.

There were a number of other successful missions in the area, most notably that of the White Fathers working among the Bemba. Equally there were some failures like Arnott's ill-supported group of Plymouth Brothers at Msiri's capital. But what was generally remarkable was the close and normally sensible relationship that so many of them established with the local African potentates. They were able to exercise an important influence against the less-welcome contacts with the Arab and Portuguese traders. In the end they invited and welcomed the full authority of British rule but in doing so they managed north of the Zambesi to avoid the excesses that accompanied the establishment of Cecil Rhodes' mastery south of the river.

55   An industrious lady missionary of the late nineteenth century, and her helper

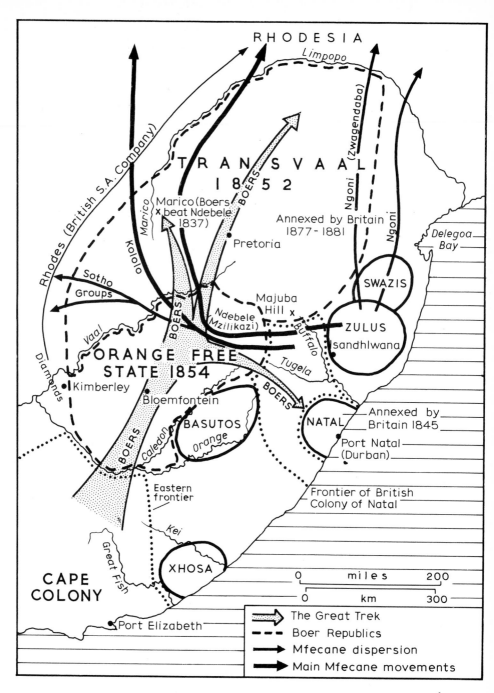

RHODESIA

Limpopo

Rhodes (British S.A. Company)

Ngoni (Zwagendaba)

T R A N S V A A L
1 8 5 2

Marico (Boers
x beat Ndebele
1837)

Marico

Kololo

Pretoria

Annexed by Britain
1877 - 1881

Ngoni

Ngoni

Delegoa
Bay

Sotho
Groups

Majuba
Hill x

SWAZIS

Ndebele
(Mzilikazi)

Vaal

BOERS

BOERS

ZULUS

Isandhlwana

Buffalo

Diamonds

ORANGE FREE
STATE 1854

Tugela

BOERS

Kimberley

Bloemfontein

BASUTOS

Orange

Caledon

NATAL

Annexed by
Britain 1845

Port Natal
(Durban)

BOERS

Eastern
frontier

Frontier of British
Colony of Natal

Kei

XHOSA

Great Fish

CAPE
COLONY

0	miles	200
0	km	300

Port Elizabeth

The Great Trek
Boer Republics
Mfecane dispersion
Main Mfecane movements

5 Southern Africa

UNTIL RECENTLY MOST histories of Africa south of the Zambesi have concentrated on the development of the white settler societies since this was the obvious feature distinguishing the region from the rest of the continent. The importance of this theme was underlined at the very beginning of the nineteenth century by the imposition in 1806 of British rule over the Afrikaner Boers, which led to a series of crises culminating in the South African War.

However significant the white presence has been, the fact remains that in 1800 Europeans occupied a relatively confined area and represented a small fraction of the total population. When the Dutch first landed at the Cape during the seventeenth century they met only the primitive Bushmen and Hottentots. It was some years before they realized that north of the Great Fish and Orange rivers were well-developed Bantu societies, culturally a part of the wider African continent. These Bantu were the southern extremity of a slow advance of population that had stretched over several centuries. During the first half of the nineteenth century that southwards progress was to be halted and actually reversed, less because of the European presence than because of the rise of the militant Zulu nation.

The result of this was that the history of southern Africa during the nineteenth century was one of conflict and disturbance as white not only clashed with white and African with African but both collided with each other. Like the United States at the same time, southern Africa had an ill-defined and moving frontier. In America, however, the Indians were a declining force, whereas in southern Africa the clash was between two expanding societies, European and African. It was a situation of enormous complexity, the full effects of which were to be felt as far away as East Africa and the southern borders of Katanga.

MAP NO. 6
Southern Africa, 1800–85

56 A Hottentot rider
with his Bushman servant,
the survivors of the earliest
inhabitants of the Cape area

Population and Land

The basic problems for both the Boers and the Bantu were an expanding
population and the need for more land. Among the Nguni, the eastern
branch of the Bantu in the lowland belt between the Indian Ocean and the
Transvaal plateau, these were particularly serious. It was a temperate
region with a high annual rainfall, well suited to the large-scale cattle
grazing practised by the Nguni. It was a normally hospitable part of the
world as long as population was held in check and there was sufficient
land for cattle. But even before 1800 these conditions were changing and
there had been periodic bouts of inter-tribal fighting over grazing rights.
The result was a growing tendency for the most powerful Nguni tribes to
expand at the expense of their weaker neighbours. This trend towards
political consolidation, particularly strong among the northern Nguni in
the area of modern Natal, was reinforced by the increased ivory trade with
the Portuguese and later with the British. Anxieties over both land and
trade were the basic cause of the series of wars at the beginning of the nineteenth century from which the Zulus emerged victorious.

Although the Boer population in Cape Colony was relatively small, they
too were faced with a serious land problem. The root of this was the
peculiar Boer method of farming. Like the Bantu, they also were large-scale

cattle grazers but, since they always insisted on individual ownership, they needed an ever-increasing amount of land. There were signs that before 1800 they were beginning to look for this beyond the frontiers of the Cape. It was a trend that was to continue for the rest of the century and to bring the Boers into direct confrontation with the expanding Bantu.

There were early indications of how serious the situation was in the region bordering the Great Fish river. The southernmost branch of the Nguni, the Xhosa, had already before 1800 spilled over the river into land which the Boers had marked for settlement. The British in 1812 forcibly evicted the Xhosa who unwillingly rejoined their kinsmen in an area where there was already serious land-hunger. Inter-tribal fighting broke out, the effects being felt by the Boers as groups of Xhosa tried to retake their lost land. An attempt was then made to interpose a neutral zone between the two races, an arrangement that did little to assist the hard-pressed Xhosa whose land it once had been and which had absolutely no appeal to the Boers. In 1820 the harassed British settled some 5,000 British immigrants in the area hoping that by working smaller farms they would persuade the Boers to alter their grazing system. The experiment failed and by the 1830s most of the British settlements were abandoned in favour of the Boer type. The one important result was the founding of Port Elizabeth which, being nearer than Cape Town, only served to encourage the economic activity of the area and pressure on the Boer to move into the interior.

The Rise of the Zulus

Until the second half of the eighteenth century, the Bantu, both the Nguni groups on the coast and the Sotho on the less hospitable plateau of the interior, had lived reasonably well in settled and peaceful conditions. A report written by some survivors of a wrecked Dutch ship in 1686 emphasized the essentially congenial way of life among the Nguni:

> It would be impossible to buy any slaves there, for they would not part with their children, or any of their connections for anything in the world, loving one another with a most remarkable strength of affection . . . The kings are much respected and beloved by their subjects . . . Of their courage little can be said, as during the stay of the Netherlanders amongst them they had no wars.

The absence of major wars was the result of there still at that time being sufficient land for expansion. But that essential condition was changing during the next hundred years. By 1800 there was only one alternative. Any Nguni tribe that wanted to increase its territory could do so only at the expense of another.

In the area of modern Natal, the stronger tribes had already begun to absorb the weaker so that three powerful Nguni groups were emerging. To the north were the Ngwane under Sobhuza, further south was the territory of Zwide, ruler of the Ndwandwe, while nearer to the coast were the Mthethwa led by Dingiswayo. Conflict between them was inevitable. Soon after the turn of the century a land quarrel led to war between the Ndwandwe and the Ngwane. The latter were defeated and Sobhuza led the remnants of his people northwards where, after conquering and absorbing the local tribes, he settled in what became Swaziland.

By 1817 Zwide had established a formidable Ndwandwe confederacy over much of northern Natal and his régime seemed secure after he defeated the Mthethwa and had Dingiswayo murdered. But on the sideline was another chief prepared to reorganize the scattered Mthethwa and use his own growing tribal power to challenge Zwide's ascendancy.

Shaka was born in 1787, the son of an unimportant Nguni chief who ruled an equally insignificant tribe, the Zulus. After a disagreement with his father, he found refuge among the Mthethwa. His courage and ability as a soldier soon brought him to Dingiswayo's attention and it was with his help that Shaka became chief of the Zulus in 1816. During the war between the Ndwandwe and Mthethwa, Shaka preferred to conserve the growing strength of his tribe. By 1818 the Zulus were sufficiently powerful to demand at least a punitive raid by Zwide. The Zulus retreated into deliberately denuded land and when the dispirited Ndwandwe turned for home, Shaka attacked. His victory at the Mhlatuze river was decisive. Zwide's short-lived ascendancy was broken and within a few years Shaka was able to dominate northern Natal.

In many ways Shaka is a difficult man to assess. Physically enormous, he was vain, lonely, and cruel but an outstanding leader and organizer. It was primarily the strength of his regiments and his intelligence as a soldier that enabled him to stamp his mark on the peoples of a wide area of southern Africa. The changes that Shaka introduced into his armies were not completely new. Dingiswayo, for example, had adopted, possibly from the Sotho, the system of age-regiments which became the central characteristic of the Zulu armies. Each regiment or *impi* was recruited from a particular age-group irrespective of the places of birth. They were always kept at the ready and lived in specially built garrisons. Each soldier and *impi* necessarily owed allegiance directly to Shaka and not to any particular local chief or area.

Shaka was also instrumental in changing the actual method of fighting. He abandoned the long throwing-spear, arguing that once a soldier had thrown it, he was disarmed and therefore useless. In its place he introduced a short stabbing instrument, not unlike a sword, which could be used while fighting in close formation. H. Fynn, an English trader who lived for some years among the Zulus, told how Shaka demonstrated this new weapon to his soldiers. Taking two regiments, he armed them with reeds:

> The two regiments thus weaponed were ordered to oppose each other, the one throwing the weapon, the other rushing on and stabbing their opponents at close quarters. The result of this collision was momentous and met with Shaka's entire satisfaction, few having escaped being wounded and several lying killed.

In battle Shaka adopted a half-moon formation, the main body being reserved in the centre while the wings outflanked the enemy. In difficult terrain, such manœuvres demanded rigid discipline. Shaka in this way fashioned a formidable military instrument, the traditions of which were continued by his successors, more particularly Cetewayo. It was he who in 1879 inflicted a severe defeat on the British army at Isandhlwana.

It was through these superb regiments that the Zulu kings created a sense of loyalty and unity that was far wider than the actual Zulu tribe itself. As the youth of defeated neighbours were incorporated into age-regiments, they dedicated themselves not only to the king but to the idea of the Zulus as a nation at arms. In spite of its cruelties, it was not an entirely ignoble concept and one which in an admittedly drastic manner went some way to solving the social and economic problems of the Nguni.

The *Mfecane*

The sudden emergence of the Zulu nation led to a long period of war, disturbance, and confusion, known by the Nguni as the *mfecane* and the Sotho as the *difaqane*, the Time of Troubles. Zulu expansion caused a chain reaction over large parts of southern and Central Africa as tribes, moved by fear and aggression, collided with each other. Contemporary accounts by missionaries and Boer trekkers tell of vast areas depopulated and grazing grounds left vacant. Once the security of tribal life was destroyed, scattered bands of marauders and bandits added to the tension. Yet, in spite of the hardship, it is possible to exaggerate the worst effects of the *mfecane*. Some of the tribes had only taken temporary refuge from the troubles in the more inaccessible parts of the country while others, gathering in heterogeneous groups under makeshift leaders, gravitated to the peripheral areas of the veld where they laid the foundations of new and often vigorous Bantu nations. Both the negative and positive aspects need to be considered in any assessment of the *mfecane*, a revolutionary situation by the side of which the Boer treks seem almost insignificant.

It was the Nguni themselves who felt the first effects. Although the Ngwane had moved north before the rise of Shaka, the formative years in the creation of the Swazi nation under Sobhuza and his son Mswati were those when the Zulus were at their strongest. More dramatic was the fortune of the defeated remnants of the Ndwandwe. Two groups fled northwards, one, under Soshangane, Zwide's senior commander, settling

57   An early photograph of

in southern Mozambique. The other, known as the Ngoni, were led by Zwangendaba through part of Mozambique, along the Limpopo and then across the Zambesi, finally settling in the Lake Nyasa area. These were the Ngoni who conquered the Malawi tribes and fought and were repulsed by the Bemba. A breakaway section pushed on still further into East Africa where they became the not wholly trustworthy allies of Mirambo. At the same time, another Ngoni group, the Maseko, moved past the east of Lake Nyasa, eventually settling in the south of modern Tanzania.

This complete reversal of the age-old Bantu advance was remarkable not just because of its effects on the other tribes it met but also for the manner in which Zwangendaba held his people together on a journey of over 2,000 miles. As he fought his way north, he not only left a trail of destruction, scattering among others the Rwozi, heirs to the great Mwenemutapa empire of the fifteenth and sixteenth centuries, but he recruited the remnants into his own age-regiments. Zwangendaba may have rejected the over-rule of Shaka but he adopted much of the disciplined organization of the Zulus. In the last analysis it can be argued that these qualities infected the conquered tribes of the Lake Nyasa region with some sense of order at

a group of Zulu warriors

a time when they were seriously threatened by slave and ivory hunters.

Other Nguni tribes fled westwards from Shaka over the Drakensberg range into the area of the present Orange Free State. Their arrival totally disrupted the Sotho people of the region, setting off tribal movements of bewildering complexity. One group in particular, the Tlokwa, led by Queen Mma Ntatisi and later by her son, Sikonyela, became the most infamous of the many marauding bands of pillagers that marched and counter-marched over the veld.

In spite of devastation of this nature, the positive aspects of the *mfecane* were already beginning to emerge. At the time when the Swazi nation was in the process of formation and the Ngoni were settling round Lake Nyasa, other groups were being welded together into relatively stable societies. Not all of them were strong enough to withstand the pressures of the time. Sebitwane, for example, who led the Sotho-speaking Kololo as far as the upper Zambesi was able to establish only a short-lived dominion over the Lozi. He had conquered one of the best-organized people of Central Africa and, as the Kololo themselves were weakened by the blandishments of the slavers from Angola, his régime collapsed after his death in 1851. Even so, Sebitwane's achievement in maintaining the coherence of his people over many years and during a long and difficult journey, deserves comparison with that of Zwangendaba.

A more successful achievement was the creation of Matabeleland in modern Rhodesia, which only succumbed before the Maxim guns of Rhodes' British South Africa Company during the 1890s. The inspiration here was a small Nguni tribe, the Ndebele.[1] Their leader, Mzilikazi, was a bold and imaginative soldier, one of the few hereditary chiefs whom Shaka promoted to be a commander. In 1821, resenting and fearing the Zulu king's authority, he led a small but tightly organized group of Ndebele into the Transvaal where he violently disrupted the lives of the local Sotho and Tswana tribes. As with the other Nguni refugee groups, survival depended not just on military skills but also on their ability to graft non-Ndebele elements to the original nucleus. Mzilikazi was highly successful in this and many of these conquered groups became his most loyal followers. The Wesleyan missionary, J. Archbell, wrote after meeting him in 1829 that

> he has obtained such authority among his people that their very senses are influenced by him; so that nothing delights his people that does not delight him and if he is well pleased his people are in ecstasy.

[1] In Sotho, the Matabele.

58 A Ngoni warrior, from a painting by
Sir Harry Johnston

Circumstances demanded that Mzilikazi constantly showed his strength and as a result he has had a reputation as cruel and savage. But it is difficult to believe that he could have welded together so many disparate groups simply by brutal methods. There is sufficient evidence to suggest that he was capable of good judgement and compromise. Robert Moffat, the Scottish missionary who knew him better than any other European, recalled how a subsidiary chief was brought before him charged with not attacking some itinerant marauders. The unfortunate man defended himself with spirit and as a result became a firm ally and friend of Mzilikazi who told him, 'You have spoken what your heart feels: go in peace. You shall not die but live while I live.'

The Ndebele remained in the Transvaal from 1823 to 1837, attacked by a number of enemies including the Boers who were beginning to infiltrate into the area. It was after a particularly heavy Boer attack that Mzilikazi took the Ndebele north over the Limpopo on to the Rhodesian plateau where they conquered and absorbed the Shona. It was a tribute to their régime in what became known as Matabeleland that one of the Shona motives in supporting the Ndebele revolt of 1896–97 against Rhodes' Company was their preference for the rule of Mzilikazi and his successor Lobengula.

59 Moshesh, creator and defender of the Basuto nation

106

Far to the south at the other end of the veld there was emerging another new nation, Basutoland. The area between the Orange and Caledon rivers was rough and mountainous, providing ideal defensive positions for those who were able to use them. Throughout the *mfecane*, frightened remnants of the southern Sotho and others were attracted there, not least because of the reputation of Moshesh. The chief of an unimportant tribe, he had by the middle of the century transformed the shattered and dispirited survivors under his rule into a cohesive unit. His achievement was the greater in that he had to deal not only with the predatory stragglers of the *mfecane* but also with the more efficiently organized Boers and British. Eugène Casalis, the French missionary who became his friend and adviser, wrote:

> Desolation was carried into the peaceful valleys of the Lesuto, fields remained uncultivated, and the horrors of famine were added to those of war. Nearly all the influential men in the country were swept away by the tide of war. Moshesh breasted the storm. Being of a very observant disposition, he knew how to resist and how to yield at the right moment; procured himself allies, even among the invaders of his territory; set his enemies at variance with each other, and by various acts of kindness secured the respect of those even who had sworn his ruin.

Moshesh established himself in the mountain stronghold of Thaba Bosiu where he beat off successive attacks from the Tlokwa, the Ndebele of Mzilikazi, and the half-caste Griquas. He was faced too with the Boers pushing over the Orange river and inevitably there were clashes over grazing lands and boundaries. The British were forced to take note of these problems without always being able to act decisively. It was a difficult position calling for tact and diplomacy from Moshesh. The British were impressed. Sir Harry Smith, one of the Cape governors, described him as 'a very superior man, possessing a strong mind adapted for government'.

Smith's tribute was justified both by the manner in which Moshesh dealt with his external enemies and by his successful uniting of his ill-assorted subjects. He argued that many of them were simply the victims of circumstances and that given the opportunity to rehabilitate themselves they would prove loyal subjects. Against the advice of his chiefs, he treated some of the bandit elements liberally and was proved correct in his judgement. Given the different tribal groups under his authority, Moshesh was forced to allow more decentralization than was normal among the Nguni-inspired nations. But this was part of the sharp contrast between a régime like that of Shaka which was geared to war and expansion and his own which, though ready and able to defend itself, was essentially a haven of security and peace.

Moshesh died in 1868 having spent the last years of his life in interminable fighting and wrangling with the Boers. The centrifugal elements in the still young Basuto nation might have destroyed all that he had accomplished, but the continued white pressure combined with the traditions he had established preserved the unity of the new state. In 1884 the British established Basutoland as a Crown Colony, entirely separate from the Cape. The next year saw similar protection extended to Bechuanaland where the expansion of some of the Tswana chiefdoms had provided another example of political amalgamation. Finally, in 1903, Swaziland was taken over by Britain but again having no connection with the Cape. In all these cases, the British action, besides preventing these new nations being submerged by the Boers, was an unwitting tribute to the considerable achievements of some great African leaders.

The Great Trek

The various British governors at the Cape knew little about the nature of the *mfecane*, though, as the Boers advanced beyond the Orange river, they could not ignore its consequences. Officials in London tended to see the Cape largely as a half-way house to India and to regard the business of the interior as confusing and irritating. James Stephen in 1841 acidly summed up the British view when he suggested there was little reason for spending large sums of money on people 'as numerous as the inhabitants of one of the second rate towns of England'.

In practice, however, the issues in southern Africa were a great deal larger than many officials in London realized. The chief one remained that of land. Britain's efforts to settle the eastern boundary question had displeased the Boers who were even more irritated in 1836 when London insisted that that land beyond the Great Fish river that had been annexed by the Cape should be returned to the Africans. The eastern outlet, however, was effectively blocked while that to the north-west was barren and arid. The only prospect seemed to be the route north over the Orange river. Great expectations were felt by a reconnaissance in 1834 that pushed

60   Under a succession of able commanders, the
Zulus dominated Natal until the 'imperial factor',
in the shape of the not always victorious British
army, finally defeated them

up into the Transvaal and as far as Natal and reported on the large areas of
vacant grazing land. Pioneer bands had for some years been probing over
the frontier. To Dr John Philip of the London Missionary Society the
consequences were obvious. They were 'like to breaking out of water,
although that nearest the break runs first, that behind, even to the extremity of the dam, soon follows'.

The land issue was the major cause of the Boer advance known as the

61 A Boer farmer of the early nineteenth century.
The substantial, Dutch-style house overlooks prosperous grazing lands

'Great Trek' but it was not the only one. Many Boers felt a deep suspicion of British authority especially as the officials in London had the ear of the powerful missionary lobby. The crucial problem was that of race relations. The missionaries, headed by the influential Dr Philip, were appalled at the Boer attitude to the Africans which appeared to condemn them to a perpetual role as hewers of wood and drawers of water. British legislation in the early years of the century tried to inject a note of responsibility, culminating in the so-called 'Black Circuit' to investigate complaints by African servants against their white masters. The unfortunate conclusion to this was the Slachter's Nek rebellion of 1815 on the eastern frontier following the death of a Boer who had resisted arrest. Although easily squashed, it left a note of deep resentment since five of the ringleaders were hanged in gruesome circumstances.

The bitterness of the Boer reaction to Britain's attitudes was under-standable but it did less than justice to the views of many British officials in the Cape. They were aware of the complicated nature of the problems they faced and were consequently often irritated at missionary behaviour, especially that of Dr Philip, some of whose reports they knew to be in-accurate and exaggerated. Nevertheless, they could not be other than sympathetic to the broad outlines of the missionary case especially when it was supported in London by a number of influential figures. In 1828, therefore, the Cape officials took the initiative in passing the Fiftieth Ordinance giving the Cape Hottentots and other Africans there equal protection at law with Europeans. In 1833 slavery was abolished throughout the whole British empire leading in the Cape to some unfortunate disputes about compensation. Anna Steenkamp, sister of one of the Great Trek leaders, commented that what really hurt was less the slaves obtaining their freedom than their being placed

> on an equal footing with Christians, contrary to the laws of God and the natural distinction of race and religion . . . wherefore we rather withdrew in order then to preserve our doctrines in purity.

The Great Trek began in 1836 and during the next ten years or so some 10,000 Boers left the Cape. They went normally in small parties made up of family groups. The less brave settled on the borders of Griqua territory and Basutoland but the majority pushed on to the north. Andries Potgieter led some of the trekkers into the Transvaal where they forced the Ndebele over the Limpopo. A larger party under Piet Retief made for Natal where a small European trading settlement already existed on the coast. This move enabled the Boers to by-pass the Xhosa and occupy some of the best

62   An early photograph of a Boer ox-waggon, typical of the kind used in the Great Trek

farming land in the region. It also made them the neighbours of the Zulus. Dingaan, alarmed at the arrival of the Boers, succeeded in tricking and murdering Retief. This was the signal for a short but fierce war during which the Boer leader, Andries Pretorius, defeated the Zulus at Blood river in December 1838. The shock of failure led to a bitter feud and civil war among the Zulus, a quarrel carefully encouraged by the Boers who were as a result able to consolidate their new republic in Natal.

The British were far from happy about the results of the Great Trek. They were particularly alarmed by the presence of a viable Boer state directly on the sea-coast and in 1845 they annexed Natal. The majority of the frustrated Boers then retreated inland where two other republics were in the process of being established, the Orange Free State and the Transvaal. The British found their existence annoying but they were landlocked and therefore dependent in the last analysis on the Cape. Accordingly, Britain recognized their independence, the Transvaal at the Sand River Convention (1852) and the Orange Free State at the Bloemfontein Convention (1854).

The Emergence of South Africa

The Great Trek holds a central position in Afrikaner mythology. No other part of their history illustrates so well their peculiar national self-confidence, their Calvinistic belief that God has guided them and saved them, the fact that, by ridding themselves of an alien rule, they could live according to their own particular precepts. For the Trek was not simply an acceleration of the slow-moving frontier but a conscious and determined effort to secede from British rule. There was a sense in which the hardy Boer farmers welcomed the hostile environment since they could shape it as they willed and not according to the unsympathetic dictates of British officials and missionaries.

In practice, however, the new republics were far from viable and this was a matter of grave concern to the British. Neither of them was wealthy nor were they in the early days able to conduct their internal affairs without bitter rivalry. At worst, as in the Transvaal, this led to a civil war, at best, as in the Orange Free State, it meant that the burghers were unable to leave their farms for more than three days to attend parliament. There was little money for administrative purposes and the likelihood of increasing revenue anywhere in southern Africa seemed improbable after the opening of the Suez Canal in 1869.

Ineffective control meant that there was no power to stop raiding on the ill-defined frontiers with the Bantu tribes. The Boers had the advantage of weapons and the knowledge that if the worst happened the British would step in to save the day. But even that did not prevent some spectacular African triumphs. Isandhlwana in 1879, when the Zulus destroyed a British force, was the most famous. But it proved a transitory victory and in 1887 Zululand accepted British authority. The resistance of the Basutos to pressure from the Orange Free State was aided by Britain's unwillingness to hand the area over to the republic and by Moshesh's uncanny skill at playing the British and Boers off against each other.

The clash between the trekkers and those Bantu disturbed by the *mfecane* was unavoidable. Many Africans resisted the Boer advance and determined the pattern of its development. Others, already disorientated by the tremendous events of the *mfecane*, were too weak and succumbed to the superior armaments of the white settlers. One disagreeable consequence was the extension to many of the Bantu of the racial prejudices of the Boers. In the Cape, the Fiftieth Ordinance had won general if sometimes reluctant acceptance. This was not so elsewhere, not even in Natal with its mainly British population. In the Boer republics racial tensions were further increased by the constant frontier fighting. Livingstone noted during the 1840s how he had seen

Boers coming to a village and, according to their usual customs, demanding twenty or thirty women to weed their gardens . . . Nor have the Boers any wish to conceal the meanness of thus employing unpaid labour; on the contrary, every one of them, from Mr Potgieter . . . downwards lauded his own humanity and justice in making such an equitable regulation. 'We make the people work for us, in consideration of allowing them to live in our country'.

The inability of the almost penniless Boer republics to control their affairs became an increasing matter of concern to the British. After the failure of an ill-conceived plan for a confederation in 1875, the Transvaal was annexed in 1877. This action could only be justified if the British were able to deal successfully with the Bantu, especially the Zulus. But Isandhlwana quickly undermined Britain's authority and the Transvaal Boers regained their independence after the British mismanaged a campaign against them that ended in defeat at Majuba in 1881.

Meanwhile, a new dimension was added to an already complex situation first by the discovery of diamonds at Kimberley during the 1870s and then of gold on the Rand in 1885. The British were able to keep the diamond-fields within their sphere of influence but the gold-workings were in the heart of the Transvaal. A large number of miners and concession-hunters rushed to the boom-town of Johannesberg, described by one Englishman as 'Monte Carlo superimposed upon Sodom and Gomorrah'. These *uitlanders* soon became the cause of serious disputes between the British and the Transvaal Boers led by the conservative and uncompromising figure of President Paul Kruger. They were neither liked nor respected and few of their demands were recognized, least of all their anxiety to have the vote. 'It is not the franchise you want but my country,' was Kruger's blunt judgement.

The basic issue, however, was less the plight of the *uitlanders* than the new-found wealth that the gold discoveries placed in the hands of the Transvaal authorities. At a time when the Germans were already occupying south-west Africa and the Boers were seeking a rail outlet to Portuguese territory, the Transvaal was emerging as a new focus of power in southern Africa. The British were faced by a crisis of the first magnitude. The root cause of the situation that led to the outbreak of the Boer War in 1899 was

63 *Uitlanders*, braving every discomfort, on their way to the gold fields of the Rand

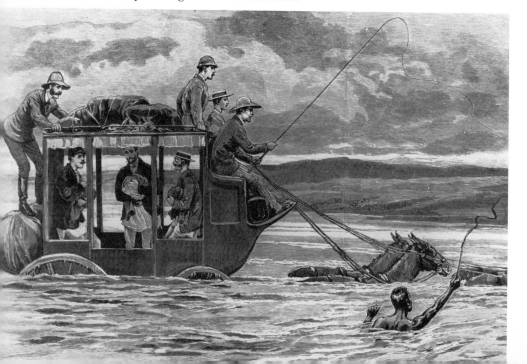

64 Boers of three generations photographed
during the Boer War (1899–1902)

the issue of paramountcy. On whose terms was the area to be administered,
those of Britain or those of the potentially rich and therefore powerful
Transvaal?

The British had one slender advantage. In 1872 the Cape had been
granted responsible government and within that framework there grew up
a working alliance between liberal Boers and the British. This became the
basis of the government which Cecil Rhodes formed in 1890. The most
influential figure in South Africa, Rhodes was an Englishman who had
made his fortune at the diamond-mines and who believed that wealth was
the precondition of power. For Rhodes everything had its price and he
usually could afford to pay for it. He once seriously asked Charles Stewart
Parnell, currently involved in his famous divorce scandal, why he could
not square the Pope. In 1885 Britain had secured 'the missionary road',
the route north through Bechuanaland. It was along this route that Rhodes'
British South Africa Company advanced into what became Rhodesia in
the hope of finding gold in sufficient quantity to act as a counter-balance
to the Transvaal. The responsibility borne by Rhodes was enormous.

Olive Schreiner commented just before he became the Cape premier:

> The only big man we have here is Rhodes and the only big thing the Chartered Company. I feel a nervous and almost painfully intense interest in the man and his career. I am so afraid of his making a mistake . . . I don't see how he can play the hand of the Chartered Company and the hand of the Colony at the same time.

She was right in expressing such reservations. Whatever small hope there was of a settlement was to be ruined by Rhodes' monstrous ambitions.

In Rhodesia, the Chartered Company was involved during 1896–97 in the serious revolt of the Ndebele and the Shona although north of the Zambesi its ambitions were limited by the Colonial Office presence. Not only had Rhodesia involved Rhodes in some serious fighting but it had also disappointed him in that gold was not found in the expected quantity. It was the genesis of his gravest error. The idea of using the *uitlander* grievances in the Transvaal to allow an invasion by the Chartered Company's forces could hardly have been justified even if it had succeeded. The failure, however, of the Jameson Raid in 1895 was a tragedy for South Africa. It put the Transvaal Boers morally in the right and pushed the hesitant Orange Free State into Kruger's arms. Anglo-Boer co-operation in the Cape collapsed and Rhodes was forced to resign as prime minister. Nor was a delicate situation improved by the appointment as High Commissioner in 1897 of Sir Alfred (later Lord) Milner who proudly announced that he was 'an imperialist out and out'. Neither Milner nor Kruger were flexible enough to be able to rescue South Africa from a century of suspicion and from the particular consequences of Rhodes' ambitious follies.

The Boer War lasted almost three years and the ultimate British victory was never in doubt although Boer tactics provided some embarrassing defeats for the unimaginative British commanders. Peace was concluded in May 1902 at the end of a war that had solved nothing as the more percipient politicians had realized before it had actually started. One of them, Hicks-Beach, told the British cabinet, 'If the Boers resist and are beaten, they will hate us still more'. The reaction of a liberal Boer like J. C. Smuts was typical. 'One becomes sick and tired of life's toil and endless endeavours. Ever since the war I have been in this mood of ennui.' The Boers were especially angry at Milner's scheme to encourage large-scale British immigration to swamp the Afrikaner element in the Transvaal. His attempts to tamper with their educational system met bitter resentment particularly

65 President Kruger and his wife. He
accurately personified the stubborn Calvinistic
virtues of the Boer people

since he tried to insist that 'Dutch should only be used to teach English and English to teach everything else.'

Such drastic solutions were rejected by the new Liberal government in Britain after the 1906 election. In that year the Transvaal and Orange Free State were given responsible government. Smuts, who was closely involved in the negotiations, was deeply moved. 'They gave us back in everything but name, our country. After four years! Has such a miracle of trust and magnanimity ever happened before.' Balfour, the Opposition leader in Britain, was less impressed, castigating the Liberal gesture as 'the most reckless experiment ever tried in the development of a great colonial policy'. His worst fears were realized when the Transvaal elected a Boer

66 & 67 The opposing sides at the siege of Ladysmith during the Boer War. The Boers proved themselves superb soldiers and only

ministry in 1907, the same happening the next year in the Orange Free State and in the Cape in 1908. Only in Natal was there a British-based administration. The Boers, having lost the war, had won the peace. Their victory was completed by the Act of Union in 1910 when the constitution was so designed that it favoured the Afrikaner elements in the new state.

The basic premise of the Liberal policy and that of the Boer leaders like Smuts and Louis Botha, the first premier of the Union, was the assumption that the foundations had at last been laid for a long period of Anglo-Boer co-operation. But in practice this was based on a fatal error. To achieve this white unity it had been necessary to sacrifice the major political rights of the Africans. This was the only consideration on which practically every

during the last eighteen months of the war were
the superior capabilities of the Imperial forces
used to any advantage

European in South Africa was agreed. As early as 1897 Milner had realized this. He wrote to Asquith:

> I remain firmly of the opinion that if it were not for my having some conscience about this treatment of the blacks, I *personally* could win over the Dutch in the Colony and indeed in all the South African dominions . . . and that I could do without offending the English. You have only to sacrifice 'the nigger' absolutely and the game is easy.

After the war, he commented again on 'the extravagance of the prejudice on the part of almost all the whites – not the Boers only – against any concession to any coloured man'. In the long debates on the Act of Union in the British Parliament few made any reference to the price that was being paid to unite the two white races. An exception was one of the small group of Labour members, Keir Hardie, who told the Commons:

> For the first time we are asked to write over the portals of the British Empire – Abandon hope all ye who enter here.

68 Although they rarely enter the picture, Africans were used by both sides for carrying supplies in the Boer War. This figure of a British soldier was carved by an African observer

120

6 The Scramble for Africa

DURING THE TWENTY or so years after 1880 most of Africa was partitioned among the European powers. The explanation of this scramble for tropical African territory is complicated and controversial. A number of answers have been advanced and common to most of them has been the view that the solution was to be found in the end in Europe. This bias still remains largely valid although in recent years arguments have been put forward to suggest that events in Africa itself were more important than had previously been recognized. Certainly, it is no longer possible to regard the Africans as the idle and helpless recipients of European rule since it is now clear that many of them showed considerable initiative in shaping the actual course of the scramble.

Africa and Imperialism

One particular argument can now be discounted as far as tropical Africa is concerned. It is the view associated most notably with J. A. Hobson and V. I. Lenin who were anxious to formulate a general theory of imperialism. Briefly, they argued, colonial ventures were the result of late nineteenth-century capitalism. It was assumed that there was chronic under-consumption and that wealth was so unequally distributed that the working classes were deprived of the means of buying. The capitalists, finding few profitable areas of investment in their domestic economies, were forced to look abroad to colonies instead. The British radical, H. N. Brailsford, expressed this more pungently:

> Working men may proceed to slay each other in order to decide whether it shall be French or German financiers who shall export the surplus capital (saved from their own wages bill) destined to subdue and exploit the peasants of Morocco.

Unfortunately for this argument there is little evidence of large-scale financial investment in tropical Africa either during or in the immediate aftermath of the scramble. What there was went in the main to southern Africa, attracted by the rich mineral deposits of South Africa, the Rhodesias, and Katanga.

In rejecting a large and grandiose theory of this nature there is the attendant danger of ignoring economic arguments altogether. There were some who had firmly convinced themselves that Africa would be a profitable field for investment. Cecil Rhodes was always a bold financial calculator as was Leopold II of the Belgians. Nevertheless, Rhodes' British South Africa Company paid no dividends before 1923 while Leopold II went bankrupt as a result of his Congolese ventures.

On a more realistic level there were those who saw tropical Africa as a source of raw materials and a market for domestic manufactures. Again, many were to be disappointed in their often modest hopes but they were men not without influence back in Europe. These trading expectations were partly a legacy of the earlier part of the century when it had been confidently believed that legitimate trade would end the traffic in slaves. Livingstone emphasized constantly the connection between Christianity and commerce as combining a noble motive with profitable enterprise. Rhodes, more typically, could talk of 'philanthropy plus 5 per cent'.

69   A cartoon of Leopold II's despairing efforts to extract rubber from his Congolese possessions

In Europe there were a good many commercial houses prepared to explore the possibilities of African trade. In Zanzibar during the 1870s Germans were as active in trading as the British. The same was true of the British and French in West Africa. Sir George Goldie, founder of the Royal Niger Company, wrote of the Niger area in 1885:

> With old-established markets closing to our manufactures, with India producing cotton fabrics not only for her own use but for export, it would be suicidal to abandon to a rival power the only great remaining undeveloped opening for British goods.

Often the governments at home remained unconvinced though both Britain and Germany were prepared to encourage chartered companies like Goldie's or Rhodes', but on the understanding that they relied on their own resources. In the end these companies normally had to be rescued by government action but the significant point was that their promoters genuinely believed in the commercial possibilities of Africa.

Equally important but less easy to define was the growth of informed public opinion about the African continent. The often extraordinary journeys of the explorers – Burton, Speke, Grant, Livingstone, Stanley,

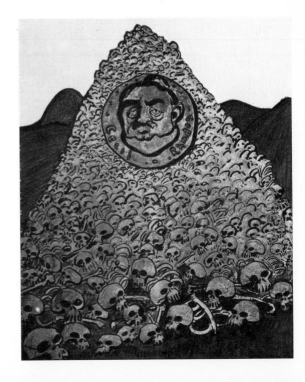

70 A French caricature of the rich and ambitious Cecil Rhodes, who dominated the period of the scramble

Barth, de Brazza, and others – nourished this interest as did the propaganda of the different missionary organizations.

In the main the views expressed about Africa in the 1860s and 1870s were in the tradition of the earlier British humanitarians who had campaigned against the slave trade. What was demanded was less physical occupation than an extension of legitimate trade and the furtherance of missionary work. This was the purpose of Livingstone's dramatic appeal to the Cambridge undergraduates in 1857:

> I go back to Africa to try to make an open path for commerce and Christianity. Do you carry out the work which I have begun. I leave it with you.

But thirteen years later at Oxford, John Ruskin was introducing a far more strident note.

> Will the youths of England make your country again a royal throne of kings, a sceptered isle, for all the world a source of light, a centre of peace? . . . This is what England must either do or perish: she must found colonies as fast and far as she is able, formed of her most energetic and worthiest men; seizing every piece of fruitful waste ground she can set her foot on, and there teaching these her colonists . . . that their first aim is to be to advance the power of England by land and sea. . . .

Such a message made an instant impact on the young Rhodes when he arrived at Oxford in 1873. Nor were such views unknown in other parts of Europe. Tennyson's fear that England might become 'some third-rate isle half-lost among her seas' was echoed in the far more sophisticated arguments of the influential French economist, Paul Leroy-Beaulieu. He insisted that France must find new colonies if she was to avoid becoming as powerless as Greece or Belgium. His anxiety would have been greater had he known the full details of the ambitions of Leopold II of the Belgians, which were to lead in 1885 to the foundation of the Congo Free State.

The Role of the European Governments

In the last analysis the views of missionaries and merchants were unimportant unless they could obtain the official backing of their governments for a forward policy in Africa. Rarely, however, before the early 1880s did

71 Rhodes' only rival
was the equally un-
scrupulous Leopold II
of the Belgians

they find much enthusiasm for African ventures in the capitals of Europe
and even during the scramble itself politicians were frequently lukewarm.

The scramble itself was essentially a by-product of the European diplomatic scene following the Franco-Prussian War of 1870–71. None of the
powers, least of all the new Germany, wanted a repetition and in an effort
to ensure peace Bismarck devised a complicated alliance system embracing
Austria, Russia, and Italy. The two liberal democracies, Britain and France,
were excluded just at a time when a number of colonial differences strained
relations between them. It was a situation that Bismarck exploited to the
full and almost by accident sparked off the scramble.

Neither Britain nor France were keen on new tropical colonies although
there was a group of French politicians, led by Jules Ferry and L. M.
Gambetta, who were convinced that an imperialist policy was the best way
of diverting public opinion from the 1870–71 defeat. As Gambetta saw it,
colonial expansion would be 'the first faltering steps of her convalescence'.
It was an attitude that Bismarck encouraged but, perhaps because it
received such obvious German support, other French politicians remained unconvinced and consequently there was never a coherent French
overseas policy. In Britain the official attitude still reflected that of the 1865

Select Committee that had recommended a withdrawal from most of the British commitments in West Africa. The fact that the 1865 report had not been implemented did not alter the general view that new colonial responsibilities in Africa were not wanted.

What changed the situation was the increasing Anglo-French rivalry in West Africa between different groups of traders during the 1870s and their extending commercial involvement with the Africans. The French colony of Senegal had been firmly secured under the governorship of Louis Faidherbe (1854–65) who had begun to push inland towards the upper Niger. Nobody in London was very concerned about this until Gladstone's unexpected and unwilling occupation of Egypt in 1882 and Leopold of the Belgians' growing interest in the Congo region during the early 1880s.

Both these events acted as a catalyst. The French were thoroughly irritated about Egypt, which they had always regarded as being part of their sphere of influence. British attempts to make their own trading position in the Congo safer by allowing the mouth of the river to be controlled by Portugal alarmed both Leopold and France. Only Bismarck rejoiced in a situation that enabled him to show friendship to France while trying to

72 In 1882 Arabi Pasha led an unsuccessful
rebellion against Anglo-French influence in Egypt,
which resulted in British occupation

drive in more deeply the wedge between London and Paris. It fitted his calculations exactly, both diplomatic and domestic, to intervene in Africa and seize colonies for Germany, the sites of which seemed to have been specially chosen to embarrass British interests. At the same time he took the opportunity to call a conference at Berlin in 1884–85 to discuss more fully the whole problem of Africa. It was an incongruous affair. Dominated by the German chancellor who previously had shown scant interest in Africa, the conference saw Britain and France reduced almost to the status of junior partners. The ambitious Leopold obtained the vast Congo Free State and a number of general principles were laid down to govern the occupation of African territory. The conference marked the beginning of a curious exercise in cartography as colonial frontiers were drawn by men who knew little about geography and rather less about those whose allegiance they were claiming.

What suddenly sparked off the scramble then were events in West Africa, the Congo, and Egypt but there is no reason to think that they would have led to a rapid colonization of Africa unless problems in Europe had demanded it. In this sense, therefore, the scramble was simply an extension of European diplomacy, a form of safety-valve diverting attention from more serious areas of crisis such as the Balkans or Alsace-Lorraine. This is presumably what Bismarck meant when he announced in 1888 that 'my map of Africa lies in Europe. Here is Russia and here lies France; that is my map of Africa.' Some justification of this view is to be found in the general increase of European tension that followed the settlement of outstanding colonial differences between Britain, France, and Russia after 1905. At the same time there were obvious dangers in using colonial affairs in this way. There was always the possibility that a colonial quarrel in Africa or elsewhere might get out of hand and become a European one, as almost happened during the Anglo-French crisis at Fashoda in 1898. It may be that the failure of African rivalry to lead to a major European confrontation merely reinforces the view that most of the statesmen involved found their new colonial commitments essentially trivial.

The fact that so few European politicians in the 1880s had any real interest in Africa is perhaps the most remarkable commentary on the whole business of the scramble. Most would have shared Gladstone's boredom when he referred to Mount Kilimanjaro as 'that mountain with the unpronounceable name'. By the 1890s there was a semblance of change, particularly in Britain. Joseph Chamberlain, Colonial Secretary from 1895

73 H. M. Stanley, through
whose agency Leopold II
established claims along
the Congo basin, forming the
nucleus of the Congo Free State

to 1903, backed Lugard and the Royal Niger Company in their occupation of the north Nigerian hinterland as well as helping to precipitate the Boer War. In their different ways Lords Salisbury and Rosebery rescued the British position in East Africa by ensuring that they controlled the Nile from its headwaters in Uganda to Egypt. But even here the motive was less a desire for more African territory than the strategic view that control of the Nile was necessary for the proper security of the Suez Canal. In this successful defence against the French threat across the Sahara the British were aided by the singular lack of interest at Berlin in her own East African territories that enabled treaty arrangements to be drawn up to Britain's advantage.

Only one European statesman showed any real eagerness in his approach to Africa, Leopold II, and even here he acted in a private capacity without any overt support from the Belgian government. His motives were complex and often obscure. Rhodes, with whom he had much in common, met him only once and was heard to mutter as he left, 'Satan, I tell you that man is Satan.' Through the agency of H. M. Stanley, Leopold established claims along the Congo basin that formed the nucleus of the Congo Free State. Originally his interests were philanthropic but these never prevented the Congo from becoming a vehicle for his own frustrations as king of neutral Belgium. Unfortunately, it proved too enormous an undertaking and in the end ruined Leopold's reputation and lost him a fortune.

The Scramble in Africa

By the mid 1880s the pattern of partition had begun to emerge. Salisbury expressed his policy as 'all British from the Cape to Cairo', an aim that was fulfilled except for the German interruption in Tanganyika. The key area was Uganda, made a protectorate in 1894. The administration of this area, including Kenya, was left in the hands of Sir William Mackinnon's Imperial British East Africa Company, a cheap method of avoiding a direct drain on the British Treasury. A similar device was used to the south when Rhodes' company was granted a charter. Around Lake Nyasa, however, the missionaries and traders were as actively hostile to Rhodes' company as they were to Portuguese advances and persuaded the government to form a protectorate in 1891.

In West Africa, British penetration came too late to save the hinterlands of Gambia and Sierra Leone from the French. But in the Gold Coast and Nigeria, the active proddings of Joseph Chamberlain and the resourcefulness of a number of men on the spot prevented the northern regions falling to the advancing French.

74 An African view of a British officer in Kenya

129

German expansion on the western seaboard was confined to stretches of coast where German missionaries and traders had already been active. Two protectorates were established in 1884 over Togoland and the Cameroons although the establishment of full political control took several more years. The setting up during 1883–84 of a German colony in south-west Africa not only threatened British control of the southern coast but also involved the Germans in costly and bitter hostilities with the local Herero people. In East Africa, German merchants had for some years been active at Zanzibar but the prime mover behind German expansion was the energetic explorer Karl Peters. Realizing that the sultan's authority was weak outside the coastal strip, he made a series of treaties with the local inland chiefs. But paper treaties did not help the Germans to establish full control which was delayed by a series of rebellions until 1907.

The French area of partition was confined to West and parts of Equatorial Africa and the vast stretches across the Sahara towards the Nile valley. Salisbury was alarmed by a possible threat to the British position in Egypt, but otherwise could see no compelling reason why the French should not have the rest of the area if they wanted it. The French organized an advance on Lake Chad from the Gaboon, Senegal and the Niger, and from

75   The French advance in the Guinea Coast area. France used African mercenary troops in her penetration of West Africa

76 Karl Peters, the German explorer who effectively established German rule in East Africa

Algeria. That they took so long to establish any firm control over this region can be partly attributed to indecision in Paris but mainly to the effective opposition of the local peoples. In particular, Rabih, a former soldier of the Egyptian army, gained the respect of the French commanders when they tried to take his slave-raiding state in the Lake Chad area. It was not until 1900 that he was finally defeated and killed.

Nearer the coast, the French began to penetrate the interior of the Gaboon after 1885 and by 1893 had also established themselves firmly in French Guinea and the Ivory Coast. In that year began the conquest of Dahomey which was largely completed by 1900. But the most important French advance was down the Senegal river towards the Niger and the hinterlands of the Gold Coast and Nigeria. The British were slow to react but in part they were assisted in their tardy salvage operation by the stiff resistance of the local inhabitants. It was among the southern Mande between the source of the Niger and the basin of the upper Volta that France's most bitter opponent emerged. Samori was not only an able soldier but an effective ruler and organizer. Tactically he avoided any direct confrontation with the French and by these Fabian methods he was able to frustrate his enemy until his final capture in 1898.

77 Lord Lugard, who helped establish British rule in Uganda and Northern Nigeria, becoming Governor General of Nigeria. The concept of Indirect Rule – governing through established African institutions – owed much to him

There is a danger in viewing the European advance as little more than the physical conclusion of the cavalier cartography of the statesmen in Paris, Berlin, and London. It was far more complicated than this. Local situations and the personal whims of resident traders, missionaries, or administrators – 'insupportable pro-consuls' as Lord Salisbury one complained – often dictated the area of occupation and the line of advance. The officials at home were then left to make the necessary frontier adjustments. Local questions and at times almost parochial wishes played a significant part in the process of the scramble. It was Peters who had, almost single-handed, laid the rough foundations of German East Africa. The same was true in Togo and the Cameroons where in the short space of ten days during July 1884 and with the innocent assistance of the British, Gustav Nachtigal signed the first German treaties of protection. Lugard masterminded not only the occupation of Hausaland but decided how it should be administered. In the case of Italy, the least successful of the European powers, the transformation of a precarious foothold on the Red Sea into the colony of Somaliland owed practically everything to the initiative of a few energetic men on the spot.

The Scramble and the Africans

An equally important consideration is that of the part played in the scramble by the Africans themselves. Traditionally they have been seen as the largely unfortunate victims of superior European skills. These were not confined to the Maxim gun. There were the often bewildering effects of treaty-makers and concession-hunters and the sometimes destructive influence of merchants and missionaries. To Lobengula, the last great chief of the Ndebele, the British take-over was like a creeping paralysis.

> Did you ever see a chameleon catch a fly? The chameleon gets behind the fly and remains motionless for some time, then he advances very slowly and gently, first putting forward one leg and then another. At last, when well within reach, he darts out his tongue and the fly disappears. England is the chameleon and I am the fly.

Clearly in certain circumstances there was some advantage in collaborating with the occupying powers since resistance might mean the loss of both lands and status. A chief, however, who assisted white penetration might strengthen his position and weaken that of his enemies. Tippu Tib

78 Lobengula, the last great chief of the Ndebele, was unable to resist the advancing forces of the British South Africa Company

recognized the power of the Europeans, agreed to help, and was appointed governor of the eastern province of the Congo Free State. Msiri on the other hand was stubborn, resisted, and was as a result murdered. The same was true of the unfortunate Lobengula. Unable to restrain his regiments, he was defeated and overthrown by Rhodes' forces. The Lozi, however, co-operated and so preserved their privileged position astride important trade routes in northern Barotseland. In what became Uganda, the Ganda civil wars resulted in the imposition of British rule which honoured the existing political system to the extent that it was allowed to spread into areas previously outside Buganda's control. The Bunyoro, in contrast, resisted fiercely and little respect was shown to their less obviously impressive political institutions.

It would be easy from this to assume that resistance did not pay but the situation was not as simple as this. Much clearly depended on the local situation. It might, for example, have been very different for the Lozi had they been faced with a serious European attack or had they been less well advised by their missionary friends. There were in fact many African leaders who refused to play a passive role and who possessed enough initiative on occasions to control the pace and direction of the European advance. Collaboration obviously had its advantages but it would be wrong to conclude that resistance did not have its benefits. The most obvious example here is that of the Ethiopians who not only defeated the Italians but emerged strong enough to expand themselves. Far to the south Moshesh's successful wars against white intruders actually allowed the emergence of a new African nation at a time when others were losing their identity. In other areas resistance may have been unsuccessful but nevertheless, as happened in Hausaland as well as in Buganda, pre-scramble political structures were not only preserved but in some ways strengthened. The final wars against Ashanti seem to have increased the often lukewarm loyalty of parts of the confederacy to Kumasi, a fact belatedly recognized by the British when they restored it in 1935.

The scramble was a complex phenomenon, the culmination of several centuries of European contact with Africa. Part of the explanation must lie in Africa itself where the freedom of action often allowed to men on the spot unwillingly forced the European governments to accept commitments they frequently did not want. When the powers did show a more positive interest it was normally for reasons totally unconnected with the continent itself. In this context it is worth remembering that the scramble was not an

79 A picture of 1893, entitled *Friends*, shows troops of the B.S.A. Company with defeated Shona. Three years later the Shona rebelled with the Ndebele against company rule

isolated series of events. There were taking place at the same time scrambles among the Pacific islands and parts of South East Asia. An unsuccessful attempt was also being made to partition China, while at a slightly later date the Middle Eastern spoils were to be divided between the powers.

80 African carvings of their new rulers following the scramble. *Left*, an official of the Congo; *right*, a teacher in Nigeria

Together they marked the end of that European expansion that had begun almost 500 years earlier with the first tentative Portuguese probings down the west coast of Africa.

To many Europeans it seemed that the scramble and the subsequent imposition of colonial rule was the most significant event ever to happen in Africa. In the confident words of Sir Harry Johnston, the continent would receive the benefits of 'the white-skinned sub-species which alone has evolved beauty of facial features and originality of invention'.

But in spite of this assertive approach, the intense interest in Africa that had marked the scramble failed to survive the period of pacification. Attention was temporarily focused on the continent whenever something seemed to go wrong, as happened during the Maji Maji rebellion in Tanganyika in 1905–7 when some 70,000 Africans lost their lives, or as the iniquities of the Congo Free State régime were revealed between 1902 and 1908. Otherwise Africa tended to be forgotten and the unfortunate colonial administrators were left to fend for themselves with the minimum of financial support. To the young Richard Meinertzhagen, serving as an official after the turn of the century, it seemed like some form of confidence trick.

> Here we are, three white men in the heart of Africa, with 20 Nigger soldiers and 50 Nigger police, 68 miles from doctors or reinforcements, administering and policing a district inhabited by half a million well armed savages who have only recently come into touch with the white man ... The position is most humorous to my mind.

Starved of both money and men, the colonial rulers persuaded themselves that in safeguarding the substance of tribal life, they were in fact doing Africa a service. Unwittingly they were emphasizing that the continuity of African life and history had not been broken by the impact of colonialism and that the scramble and its aftermath were only part of a number of important developments taking place during the nineteenth century. It was the totality of these which had shaped the evolution of the emerging Africa. The shrewd Sir Harry Johnston, in spite of his sometimes overconfident tones, was perhaps more aware of these claims of Africa and the Africans than some of his contemporaries. He admitted in 1913:

> All predictions as to the future of the Dark Continent seem futile in face of the unexpected, the strange, the unlooked for which arises in Africa itself.

Acknowledgements

The author and publishers wish to record their grateful thanks to copyright owners for the use of the illustrations listed below:

    Berkeley Galleries, London, for: 14, 25, 32, 68, 74

    Church Missionary Society for: 17, 28, 29, 30, 33, 45, 46, 48, 55

    Congregational Council for World Missions for: 41

    John R. Freeman & Co. Ltd. for: 13, 59, 61

    Hamish Hamilton Ltd. for: 39, 40

    Mansell Collection for: 15, 18, 23, 31, 36, 38, 56, 60, 64, 69

    Mary Evans Picture Library for: 2, 6, 7, 12, 16, 20, 22, 37, 42, 44, 49, 52, 70, 78

    Museum voor Land-en Volkenkunde, Rotterdam, for: title page, 3

    Paul Popper Ltd. for: 9, 10, 19, 24, 26, 27, 47, 57, 62, 65, 71

    Radio Times Hulton Picture Library for: 4, 34, 54, 63, 66, 67, 72, 75, 76, 77

    Royal Geographical Society for: 5, 53, 73

    Trustees of the British Museum for: 50

Index

Printed in Great Britain by Jarrold & Sons Limited, Norwich